PART ONE

THE ROOTS OF THE CONFLICT

The city of Jerusalem, photographed in 1980

The Middle East is one of the most important regions in the history of the world. It is where human civilisation began, some 10,000 years ago. It has been the centre of many grèat empires. Important trade routes cross the region, and today it produces a sixth of the world's oil. Above all, the Middle East is the birthplace of three great religions – Judaism, Christianity and Islam – and the area at its centre is often called the holy land. For more than four thousand years the peoples of the Middle East have fought each other for control of it.

Out of those forty centuries of war, our own century has seen some of the most savage fighting in the Middle East. Much of the fighting has been for control of the holy land, between Jewish people who call it Israel and Arab people who call it Palestine.

This book is about the twentieth-century struggle between Jews and Arabs in the holy land. But because its roots are buried deep in history, we must begin the story in ancient times.

1

A HOLY LAND

Both Arabs and Jews claim to be the rightful owners of the holy land. They base their claims on the history of their peoples and on their religions.

Jews

Jews trace their history back to Abraham who, according to their Bible, lived 4000 years ago in Ur. The Bible tells how God made an agreement with Abraham by which he and his descendants would carry the message of God to the rest of the world. In return, God promised Abraham the land of Canaan for his people. Abraham's descendants duly settled in the 'promised land' of Canaan. One of them, Jacob, was also called Israel, and twelve families which descended from him were known as the Children of Israel, or Israelites.

Towards the end of Jacob's life, a famine forced the Israelites to leave Canaan and settle in Egypt. They lived there for six hundred years until in about 1300 BC the ruler of Egypt made them into slaves.

The Bible tells how the Israelites escaped from slavery after God commanded one of them, Moses, to lead his people out of Egypt into Sinai. On Mount Sinai God appeared before Moses and renewed the agreement made with Abraham. God also proclaimed the **Torah**, or teaching, which the Israelites were to use as their law.

After forty years living as nomads in the desert, the Israelites were led by Joshua into the 'promised land' of Canaan. The population of the country when they arrived included the Canaanites, the Gibeonites and the Philistines. By the tenth century BC (that is, about 3000 years ago) the Israelites had gained control over these peoples. From 1025 BC Saul, David and then Solomon ruled over a united kingdom of Israel. During Solomon's reign many fine buildings were put up in Jerusalem, the most important being the Temple.

Following Solomon's death, the united kingdom broke apart into a northern kingdom called Israel and a southern part called Judah, with Jerusalem as its capital. Eventually both kingdoms were destroyed, Israel by the Assyrians in 720 BC, and Judah by the Babylonians in 587 BC.

Their defeat by the Babylonians was a turning point in the history of the Jews, for the Babylonians took them into captivity. While in exile in Babylon, the Jews became a united community. They put together their sacred writings, such as the Torah and the Psalms, into the Bible. By the time they returned to Palestine (as Judah was called after their exile) they were deeply committed to their religion – **Judaism**. Their society was controlled by priests and their religion was based on strict observance of God's laws.

Arab shepherds outside the Christian monastery of Mar Saba, south of Jerusalem, around 1900. Mar is Arabic for 'Saint'

The Jews remained in Palestine for 600 years after returning from Babylon. They were ruled in turn by the Persians, the Greeks and finally the Romans, who invaded Palestine in the first century BC. During those years the Jews often rebelled against their foreign rulers. In AD 70 the Roman Emperor Titus suppressed a Jewish revolt with great violence and destroyed much of Jerusalem including the Temple. The Romans then expelled most Jews from Palestine, forcing them to go into exile in foreign lands. After a second and final Jewish revolt in AD 132–135 the Roman Emperor Hadrian built a new city on the ruins of Jerusalem and forbade Jews to enter it.

From then on the Jews were mostly a scattered people living all over Europe as well as in Russia and Africa. Only a few thousand remained in Palestine to preserve their religious traditions there.

Christians

At the time when the Jews were expelled from Palestine, a new religion based on the teachings of Jesus of Nazareth was slowly taking root in the Middle East.

This new religion, **Christianity**, seemed at first to be a sect of Judaism, for nearly all Jews at that time expected God to send them a Messiah, or deliverer, and Jesus claimed to be the Messiah. The new religion also seemed unlikely to last: Jesus was opposed by all the religious leaders of the time, he was betrayed by one of his followers and he was executed on a cross like a criminal. His followers, however, believed that Jesus rose from death and they proclaimed him Lord and saviour, the Son of God.

Jews denied that Jesus was their Messiah, but Christianity soon began to spread from its birthplace in Palestine. After the conversion to Christianity of the Roman Emperor Constantine in 323, Palestine gradually became Christian in character. For example, Constantine built the Church of the Holy Sepulchre at the site of the cave in Jerusalem where, according to tradition, Jesus was buried and then rose from death. His successors covered Palestine with Christian churches and monuments and, as Palestine became more Christian, its Jewish character faded.

Muslims

During the seventh century, a third major religion spread to all parts of the Middle East. This was **Islam**, which means in Arabic 'submission to God'. Its followers were known as **Muslims** – those who submit to God.

Islam was given its name by an Arab prophet, Mohammed, who was born in Mecca in 570. Muslims believe that Mohammed was the prophet of Allah, the one true God, and that the nature of Allah was revealed to him by the Archangel Gabriel. These revelations were recorded in the Koran, the holy book of Islam.

Mohammed's preaching was unpopular in Mecca and in 622 he had to leave the city with a handful of followers to live in Medina. Mohammed's flight from Mecca is known as the **Hegira**, and is the starting point of the Islamic calendar. In Medina, Mohammed built up an army and made alliances with nearby tribes. By 630 he was strong enough to return to Mecca unopposed. From then on, Islam spread rapidly. Within 200 years Muslims had conquered all the Middle East as well as North Africa.

According to the Koran, Mohammed was miraculously taken from Mecca to Jerusalem at the end of his life. From a rock on a hill in the city, Mohammed

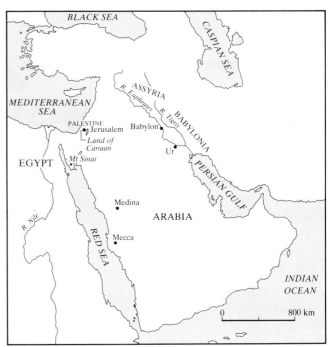

The Middle East since ancient times

ascended in seven stages to heaven.

Five years after Mohammed's death, Muslims captured Jerusalem from the Byzantines who then controlled Palestine. Jerusalem became one of the most important centres of the Islamic faith. The rock from which Mohammed rose to heaven was made the centre of a great mosque, the Mosque of the Dome of the Rock.

As a result of the Muslim conquest of Palestine, its character changed again. Like the Jews 500 years earlier, the Christians became a minority. There was a Christian revival during the Crusades of the eleventh to thirteenth centuries, but after the Muslim Arabs defeated the Crusaders in 1187 they remained the dominant people.

In 1518 the Turks conquered Palestine and made it part of the Ottoman Empire, which included most of the Middle East. However, this did not change the population of Palestine. Until 1917, when the Ottoman Empire started to break apart, the people, language, customs and culture of Palestine remained largely Arab.

Work section

A. 1. Divide a page into three columns headed 'Judaism', 'Christianity' and 'Islam'. Then put each of the following names and terms into the appropriate column. (Some should appear in more than one column.)

Allah Bible Church of the Holy Sepulchre Dome of the Rock God Jerusalem
Jesus Koran Mecca Messiah Mohammed Temple Torah

2. Using your three columns as a guide, describe (a) any similarities, and (b) any differences that you can see between the three religions.

B. Study the photograph of Jerusalem on page 1. What similar ideas and feelings might Jews, Christians and Muslims gain from this scene? How are their feelings likely to differ?

C. What does the photograph opposite reveal about Palestine at the start of this century?

3

ZIONISM AND ARAB NATIONALISM

As you have read, most Jews left Palestine after the Romans crushed their revolt in AD 70. They settled in many parts of Europe, Africa and Russia and thus became a dispersed, or scattered people.

The Jewish dispersion

Jews were badly treated in many of the countries where they settled. In some places they were not allowed to own land. In others they had to live in walled-off areas of towns known as **ghettoes**. Often they had to pay special taxes and wear special clothes. Sometimes their homes were attacked and, occasionally, they were expelled from their adopted countries.

Anti-semitism, as this ill-treatment of Jews is called, had many causes. Mistrust of foreigners, jealousy and plain cruelty all played a part. Religion also led to anti-Semitism, for many Christians believed that Jews were responsible for killing Christ. Jews were also often accused of murdering Christian children to use their blood for baking Passover bread.

Jews reacted in different ways to anti-Semitism. Some tried assimilation – that is, adopting the dress, habits, customs and language of the country in which they had settled. Some tried to get themselves accepted as Jews with equal rights. Others tried to maintain their Jewish identity by strictly following a Jewish style of life and religion.

This is what Jews in Russia had done. Russia's 4 million Jews were only allowed to live in an area called the Pale of Settlement. In the Pale, they existed as a separate society. They shared a common religion (Judaism), diet (kosher), spoken language (Yiddish) and sacred language (Hebrew) and they shared the same traditions and culture. In this way, they were not assimilated and most Russians regarded them as an alien people.

In the 1880s Russia's treatment of Jews became brutal and oppressive. People blamed them for the assassination of their ruler, Tsar Alexander, in 1881 (one of his killers was Jewish) and killed many Jews in a series of bloody attacks known as 'pogroms'.

Zionism

As a result of the pogroms, many Jews began to talk about leaving Russia. Some did so: 135,000 Russian Jews went to settle in the USA during the 1880s. Many of those who stayed in Russia joined a movement known as 'Lovers of Zion'. Their aim was to go in groups to settle in Zion, the old Jewish name for Palestine.

The first group of **Zionists**, as the Lovers of Zion were known, arrived in Palestine in 1882. They

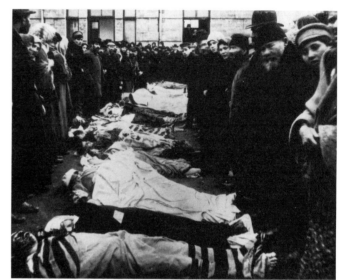

Jews awaiting burial after a pogrom in the Russian town of Odessa

founded a colony called Rishon-le-Zion (the First to Zion) near the city of Jaffa. In the same year a French Jewish millionaire, Baron Rothschild, began giving money to Zionists to help them set up more colonies in Palestine. As a result some twenty Zionist colonies had been created there by 1900.

A Hungarian Jew, Theodor Herzl, became the leader of the Zionist movement. In 1896 he wrote a book, *The Jewish State*, arguing that Jews needed their own nation state where they could escape from anti-Semitism. This state, he suggested, could be either in Palestine or in Argentina.

In 1897 Herzl organised the first Zionist Congress. This meeting of Jews from many countries decided that the Jewish state should be in Palestine and nowhere else, for that was the original home of the Jews. In 1901 the Congress set up a Jewish National Fund to buy land for Jewish settlers. As a result there were more than forty Zionist settlements in Palestine by 1914.

The Great War and Arab nationalism

When the Great War of 1914–18 began, there were about 56,000 Jews and 700,000 Arabs in Palestine. In most places they lived peaceably together. Sadly, the Great War quickly changed this situation.

The Ottoman, or Turkish, Empire which controlled Palestine, joined the war on the side of Germany and Austria-Hungary, thus becoming an enemy of Britain and its Allies. This brought Britain into alliance with the Arabs in the Ottoman Empire. Many Arabs wanted to be free from Turkish rule and thought they could become free if the Ottoman Empire was defeated in the war. They were therefore willing to help Britain fight the Turks. In a series of letters, Sherif Hussein of Mecca, the most widely recognised Muslim leader in the Middle East, agreed with Sir Henry McMahon, British High Commissioner in Egypt, that the Arabs would rebel against the Turks. In return the British, at the end of the war, would help the Arabs to form a united Arab state out of the Arab lands of the Ottoman Empire. The Arabs assumed that Palestine would be part of their new state, although the **Hussein–McMahon** letters did not state this precisely.

The Arab revolt promised by Sherif Hussein began in 1916. Helped by a British officer, T. E. Lawrence, the Arabs used guerilla warfare to tie down large Turkish forces in Arabia. In 1917 they joined up with a British army under General Allenby to capture Jerusalem. When, in 1918, they went on to capture Demascus, it seemed to the Arabs that they were about to gain their freedom.

In fact, unknown to the Arabs, the British had been playing a double game. Back in 1916 Britain and France had made a secret agreement – the **Sykes-Picot Agreement** – to divide the Ottoman Empire between them. This went against the pledges given to Sherif Hussein in the McMahon letters.

Also unknown to the Arabs was a decision by the British government to help the Zionists create a 'national home' in Palestine. The decision was contained in a letter from Arthur Balfour, Britain's Foreign Minister, to Lord Rothschild, Chairman of the British Zionists. The letter, reproduced here as source A, is known as the **Balfour Declaration**.

When they were told about the Balfour Declaration in 1918, the Arabs protested. They said that a Jewish national home could only be created at the expense of the Arabs in Palestine. In reply, the British

A. *The 'Balfour Declaration' of 1917*

> Foreign Office,
> November 2nd, 1917.
>
> Dear Lord Rothschild,
>
> I have much pleasure in conveying to you, on behalf of His Majesty's Government, the following declaration of sympathy with Jewish Zionist aspirations which has been submitted to, and approved by, the Cabinet
>
> "His Majesty's Government view with favour the establishment in Palestine of a national home for the Jewish people, and will use their best endeavours to facilitate the achievement of this object, it being clearly understood that nothing shall be done which may prejudice the civil and religious rights of existing non-Jewish communities in Palestine, or the rights and political status enjoyed by Jews in any other country".
>
> I should be grateful if you would bring this declaration to the knowledge of the Zionist Federation.
>
> Arthur James Balfour

government made further promises to help the Arabs set up a united Arab state, based on the wishes of the people. Secretly, however, the British had no intention of doing anything of the sort. In a note to the British government on 11 August 1919, Balfour wrote:

B. 'In Palestine we do not propose even to go through the form of consulting the wishes of the present inhabitants of the country . . . . Zionism, be it right or wrong, good or bad, is rooted in agelong traditions, in present needs, in future hopes, of far profounder import than the desires and prejudices of the 700,000 Arabs who now inhabit that ancient land.'

Work section

A. Test your knowledge and understanding of this chapter by explaining what the following terms mean: anti-Semitism; Zionism; the Hussein–McMahon letters; the Sykes-Picot Agreement; the Balfour Declaration.

B. Study the photograph opposite, then answer these questions:
   1. What does the photograph tell you about anti-Semitism in nineteenth-century Russia?
   2. How might such scenes have increased support for Zionism among (a) Jews, and (b) non-Jews?

C. Study sources A and B. Then, using Chapters 1 and 2 for information, answer the following:
   1. In source A, what were 'Zionist aspirations' (*Zionist hopes and aims*)?
   2. Suggest what the term 'national home' in source A means. How does its meaning differ from the word 'nation'?
   3. What are 'civil and religious rights'? Which civil and religious rights belonging to 'non-Jewish communities in Palestine' do you think the Cabinet had in mind?
   4. How might those rights be threatened by the creation of a Jewish 'national home' in Palestine?
   5. One complaint of the Arabs about the Balfour Declaration was that it called them 'non-Jewish communities'. Why do you think they objected to this?
   6. How do sources A and B suggest that the British government was pro-Zionist and anti-Arab?
   7. How reliable do you consider sources A and B as evidence of the British government's views on Palestine? Explain your answer.

THE START OF THE CONFLICT

The Great War ended in November 1918 and a peace conference was held in Paris in 1919 to decide what to do with the countries that had been beaten. As the Ottoman Empire was one of the defeated countries, the future of Palestine and its other Arab provinces was discussed at the conference.

The peace settlement in the Middle East

The peacemakers at the Paris conference decided that the peoples of defeated empires, such as the Arabs of the Ottoman Empire, should have the right of **national self-determination** – that is, the right to set up their own, self-governing, independent nations. In cases where the people had no experience of government, one of the major powers (Britain, France, the USA or Japan) would help them run their new country until they could do so themselves. A major power doing this was called a mandatory and a country it helped to run was known as a **mandate**. Every year, the mandatory would have to give a report of its activities to the League of Nations.

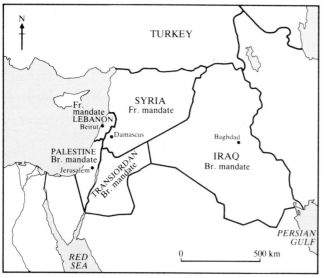

The mandates in the Middle East

Many Arabs felt in 1919 that they were capable of governing themselves, but the peacemakers did not agree. They decided that Palestine, Transjordan and Iraq should be mandates of Britain, and that Lebanon and Syria should be mandates of France.

While the peacemakers were discussing the future of the Middle East, the Zionist Organisation asked them to set up a Jewish national home in Palestine, as referred to in the Balfour Declaration. At the same time, a newly-formed Palestinian National Congress, representing Arabs, asked the peacemakers to reject the Balfour Declaration and to allow them their independence. The peace conference decided to send an enquiry team to Palestine to investigate these rival claims. The team was led by two Americans, Henry King and Charles Crane.

The **King–Crane Commission** collected many people's views on the Zionist plan for a national home in Palestine. They reported in August 1919 that:

A. '. . . the non-Jewish population of Palestine – nearly nine-tenths of the whole – are emphatically against the entire Zionist program. . . .
There was no one thing upon which the population of Palestine were more agreed than this. To subject a people so minded to unlimited Jewish immigration, and to steady financial and social pressure to surrender the land, would be a gross violation . . . of the people's rights. . . .'

The King–Crane Commission recommended that the plan should be dropped.

Nothing came of the King–Crane report. It was suppressed and kept secret for three years. Far from dropping the plan for a Jewish national home in Palestine, the peacemakers included the Balfour Declaration in the rules of the mandate by which Palestine was to be governed.

The Palestinians reacted to this by supporting Sherif Hussein, leader of the Arab independence movement since the revolt of 1917. In March 1920 a General Syrian Congress elected his son, Emir (Prince) Feisal, as king of an Arab state consisting of Palestine, Lebanon, Transjordan and Syria. The Congress which elected him issued a statement that:

B. 'We oppose the pretensions of the Zionists to create a Jewish commonwealth in . . . Palestine, and oppose Zionist migration to any part of our country; for we do not acknowledge their title but consider them a grave peril to our people from the national, economic and political points of view.'

The rule of King Feisal and the Syrian General Congress was short-lived. When Feisal started making attacks on the French, who were running Syria and Lebanon as mandates, the French army deposed him and flung him out of the country.

The British mandate in Palestine

In 1920 the British appointed Sir Herbert Samuel, an eminent British Jew and Zionist, as High Commissioner (Governor) of Palestine. Samuel's first action was to announce that 16,500 Jews would be allowed to settle in Palestine during the coming year.

Arabs protested against this and in 1921 their protests turned into riots in which forty-six Jews were killed.

An enquiry into the 1921 riots reported that they were caused by Arab dislike of the increase in Jewish immigration. Sir Herbert Samuel therefore reduced the numbers of Jews allowed to settle in Palestine. As a result, the years 1922–29 were relatively peaceful. Despite the restriction on immigration, however, sixty new Zionist settlements were created during these years and the Jewish population doubled.

In 1929 two events caused a new outburst of violence between Arabs and Jews. The first was a speech by an extreme Zionist, Vladimir Jabotinsky, in which he spoke of making Palestine into a Jewish state and of colonising Transjordan, which was closed to Jewish settlers. The second was a demonstration by extreme Zionists near the Mosque of the Dome of the Rock in Jerusalem. Arabs saw this as a threat to their religion and organised counter-demonstrations. These soon turned into mass Arab attacks on Jews throughout Palestine: 133 Jews were killed and 339 wounded.

A British enquiry into the 1929 massacre stated that:

C. 'The Palestinians have come to see in Jewish immigration not only a menace to their livelihood but a possible overlord of the future.'

Despite this, the British continued to allow Zionists to settle in Palestine. From 1933 onwards most settlers were from Germany where the anti-Semitic Nazi Party came to power in that year. With many Jews looking for an escape from Nazi persecution, the rate of immigration shot up: 30,000 in 1933, 42,000 in 1934 and 61,000 in 1935.

The General Strike of 1936

With each new wave of immigration, Arabs in Palestine began to talk of armed rebellion against British rule. In 1936 all five Arab political parties united to form the **Arab Higher Committee**, led by Haj Amin al-Husseini, the Mufti (leading Muslim priest) of Jerusalem. In May 1936 the Committee called for a general strike to protest against British rule. One of the strike organisers later recalled the aims of the strike: in an interview in 1979, he said:

D. 'Our message was simple. During the period of the Mandate the British should gradually have enabled us to move towards independence. This was supposed to be the goal of the Mandate. But it was clear that the real goal was different. It was to establish a Jewish state on our ruins, to uproot the Arabs from their country. That was how we felt, that they were going to replace us with a Jewish state.

For this reason the British were the cause of our catastrophe, and the catastrophe was Zionism. So we asked the people, "Who is your first enemy?" "Britain." "The second enemy?" "Zionism." "Why?" "Because Britain is responsible. Britain protects them and persecutes us."'

The General Strike brought Palestine to a standstill. For six months no buses or trains ran. Shops, offices, schools and factories stayed shut. In the countryside, peasants formed armed groups to fight the British army. The British mandate was under attack.

A cartoon from an Arab daily paper in 1936, comparing General Allenby, who captured Jerusalem from the Turks in 1917, with General Sir Arthur Wauchope, the British High Commissioner of Palestine in 1936

7

CHALLENGES TO BRITISH RULE

In response to the 1936 General Strike, the British set up a Royal Commission to investigate the causes of the unrest. Led by Earl Peel, the Commission reported in 1937 that:

A. 'The underlying causes of the disturbances are the desire of the Arabs for national independence and their hatred and fear of the establishment of the Jewish national home.'

Peel went on to say that Palestine should be divided into a Jewish state and an Arab state, with the British keeping control of the area around Jerusalem.

The Arab rebellion, 1937–39

The Palestinians were outraged by the Peel Report. Although Jewish settlers owned only 5 per cent of the land, Peel was suggesting that half the country should be given to a new Jewish state. As a result, the Palestinians rebelled against British rule. Armed groups blew up bridges, roads and railways, and cut telephone wires. They ambushed army patrols. They murdered British officials, policeman and soldiers.

The British army replied with tough tactics. They arrested the Arab Higher Committee (see page 7) and imprisoned thousands of Palestinians without trial. They fought the rebels with aircraft, tanks and heavy guns. They imposed collective punishments on villages which they suspected of helping the rebels and they hanged rebels caught carrying guns.

In addition to these harsh measures, the British army helped the Jews in Palestine to build up their military forces. These consisted of two secret armed groups, the **Haganah** (Defence Force) and the **Irgun Zvai Leumi** (National Military Organisation). In co-operation with the Haganah, the British organised, trained and armed a force of 14,000 men called the Jewish Settlement Police. In 1938 they also created commando units called Special Night Squads for making guerilla attacks on Palestinians.

The Arab rebellion ended in 1939, crushed by the British army. According to Britain, over 3000 rebels had been killed. The Palestinians claimed over 5000 dead. Whatever the true figure, it was a crippling blow to a people who numbered less than a million.

The 1939 White Paper

One result of the Arab rebellion was a change in Britain's immigration policy. A White Paper (a government statement of policy) in 1939 stated that Jewish immigration would be limited to 75,000 over the next five years. After five years, no more immigration would be allowed without Arab consent. After ten years Palestine would become an independent state, shared equally by Jews and Arabs.

Many Arabs felt reassured by the White Paper, but the Jews were outraged. This was just when their people were most under threat from the spread of Nazi power in Europe. In the days that followed its publication, the Irgun planted bombs and shot Arabs. It seemed that a Jewish revolt against the White Paper was about to begin.

The Second World War

In September 1939 war broke out in Europe after Germany invaded Poland. When Britain declared war on Germany, around 30,000 Jews in Palestine joined the British army: while they hated Britain's immigration policy they hated Nazi Germany more. For this reason the threatened Jewish revolt did not happen. However, David Ben Gurion, head of the Jewish Agency responsible for immigration into Palestine, said:

The Peel partition plan, 1937

B. 'We shall fight for Britain as if there is no White Paper. We shall fight the White Paper as if there is no war.'

So, while Jews fought on Britain's side in the war against Germany, they also fought against the White Paper. One way in which they did this was to smuggle Jews into Palestine by ship, avoiding the immigration authorities. Thousands of Jews were brought into Palestine in this way. On a number of occasions, however, the British stopped the ships and sent them back to where they came from – even if that happened to be in Nazi-occupied Europe. One of the ships, the *Struma*, sank after being refused permission to sail to Palestine: all but one of the 769 refugees on board were drowned.

In their fight against the White Paper, the Jews also turned for help to the USA where there was a large Jewish population. In May 1942 David Ben Gurion held a conference of leading American Zionists at the Biltmore Hotel in New York. The conference agreed on a new Zionist policy, known as the **Biltmore Programme**, calling for the immediate creation of a Jewish state in Palestine and an end to all limits on immigration.

Some extreme Zionists refused to help Britain in the Second World War. The **Lehi** (Fighters for the Freedom of Israel) saw the British as a worse enemy than Germany and used terror tactics against them. Even after their leader, Abraham Stern, was shot dead by British police in 1942, the Lehi continued to terrorise the British, murdering police as well as the Minister of State in Cairo, Lord Moyne. The Irgun also used terror against the British, blowing up government offices and killing British soldiers.

The Holocaust

As the war went on, news came out of German-occupied Europe that the Nazis were murdering huge numbers of Jews. The Jewish Agency in Palestine received reports that 1,500,000 Jews had been killed in 1943. Thousands every day were being gassed to death at Auschwitz, Chelmno, Sobibor, Maidenek, Belzec and Treblinka – camps in Poland built solely for the purpose of mass murder.

By the end of the war in 1945, 6 million Jews had died in this **Holocaust**, or mass killing. A quarter of a million who were freed from the camps had no homes to return to. This appalling tragedy aroused great sympathy for Jewish people, especially in the USA. In 1946 President Truman of the USA demanded that 100,000 Jews should be allowed into

An Irgun poster for distribution in Central Europe.

A poster of the Irgun, 1946. The Hebrew words at the top mean 'Homeland and Freedom'

Palestine at once. Britain, however, fixed the limit at 1500 a month. This was the last straw for the Zionists. The Irgun and the Lehi began a new campaign of terror against the British, but now on a larger scale. In July 1946 the Irgun blew up the King David Hotel in Jerusalem, headquarters of the British government in Palestine, killing ninety-one people.

Britain faced opposition from moderate as well as extreme Zionists. Ben Gurion and the Jewish Agency adopted a policy of opposition which involved illegal immigration on a large scale. Small ships, usually overcrowded and leaking, brought thousands of Jews from Europe to the shores of Palestine. Some sank, many were intercepted by the Royal Navy, and only twelve reached their destination. But the publicity these ships received in the world's press increased sympathy for the Jews and damaged Britain's reputation further.

Work section

A. Study the poster above, then answer these questions:
1. In what ways does the state of Israel on the poster (Erez Jisraël) differ from that recommended by the Peel Report, shown in the map opposite?
2. How would this plan for 'Erez Jisraël' have affected the Arabs of Palestine and Transjordan?
3. Suggest what is meant by the words 'The Sole Solution'.
4. Why do you think the Irgun produced this poster for distribution in Central Europe?
5. Using this poster as evidence, describe the ideas and aims of the Irgun.

5

THE END OF BRITISH RULE

By 1947 the British in Palestine were in an impossible position. Their rule was opposed by both moderate and extreme Zionists, demanding more Jewish immigration. They could not agree to those demands without angering the Palestinians. And yet, the longer they did nothing, the more violence there was. In 1946 alone there were 212 killings in Palestine – 60 Arabs, 63 Jews and 89 Britons. In April 1947 the British therefore asked the United Nations, successor to the League of Nations, to take back the mandate and to decide the future of the country.

The United Nations partition plan

In May 1947 the United Nations set up a UN Special Committee on Palestine (UNSCOP) to deal with the Palestine question. This eleven-man committee toured the Middle East, collecting evidence from Arabs and Jews. While it did so, the violence in Palestine continued, with the Irgun and the Lehi shooting and bombing both Palestinians and British. At the same time, moderate Zionists continued their campaign of illegal immigration in small ships. The most famous of these was the *Exodus*, pictured below. When the Royal Navy forced its 4500 passengers to return to the camps in Europe from which they had come, there was worldwide criticism of Britain's rule in Palestine.

UNSCOP drew up a report on Palestine in August 1947. The report said that the British mandate should end, that Palestine should be partitioned into a Jewish state and an Arab state, and that Jerusalem should be an international zone under UN control. It also proposed that the Jewish and Arab states should be linked in an economic union to help each other's trade.

The Palestinians opposed the UNSCOP plan. As you read in Chapter 4, at least 3000 Palestinians had

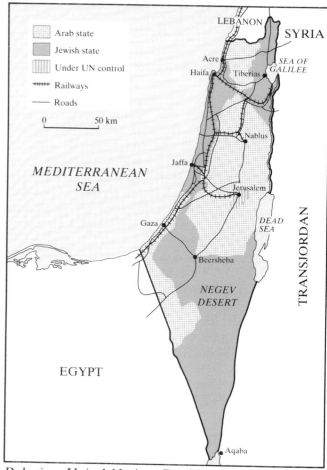

Palestine: United Nations Partition Plan, 1947

been killed fighting the Peel Plan for partition in 1937–39. You can see from the map above why they opposed it again in 1947. According to the UNSCOP plan, the Jewish state would be larger than the Arab state, even though Jews were only one third of the population and owned less than one tenth of the land.

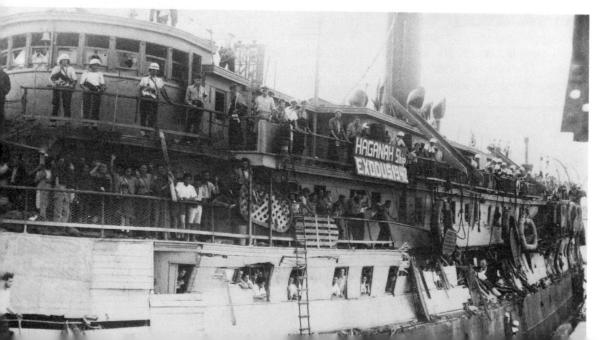

A. Exodus 1947, carrying 4500 Jews, arrives in Haifa before being forced to sail back to British-held Hamburg in Germany

The Arab state would be divided into three zones. It would have no direct access to the sea, for Jaffa, the main Arab port, would be cut off from the rest. And its land was mostly desert country which was difficult to farm: most of the fertile land, on the coast from Gaza to Acre, would be part of the Jewish state.

Despite Arab opposition, the UN voted in November 1947 to partition Palestine six months from that date. The vote was followed within days by violent Arab protests which soon turned into killings and counter-killings between Jews and Arabs.

Civil war in Palestine

As the date of partition (May 1948) drew nearer, both Jews and Arabs prepared to make war on each other. The Jews began to conscript seventeen- to twenty-five-year old men and women into the Haganah, raising its strength to nearly a million. To arm them, Haganah leaders went to the Skoda arms firm in Czechoslovakia and bought a huge quantity of armaments; 24,500 rifles, 5000 machine guns, 54 million rounds of ammunition and 25 fighter aircraft.

The Palestinians had greater difficulty in preparing for war, for their fighting strength had been virtually destroyed in 1939, when the British crushed the Arab rebellion. So they turned for help to the Arab League, an organisation of Arab states that had been created in 1945 to promote co-operation in the Arab world. The Arab League, however, could not match the strength of the Jews. It was still only a year old and its members were divided on many issues. The rulers of Saudi Arabia and Egypt were in conflict with those of Iraq and Transjordan, while the ruler of Transjordan was in conflict with Syria and Lebanon.

Despite its weaknesses, the Arab League tried to help the Palestinians. In December 1947 it declared the UN partition plan illegal and gave the Palestinians 10,000 rifles. Early in 1948 it formed an Arab Liberation Army of 3000 volunteers to fight partition.

In April 1948 full-scale civil war began between Jews and Arabs. The British, with six weeks to go before the end of the mandate, could do little to stop it. Fighting began when the Haganah launched **Operation Dalet** (Hebrew for 'D') on 4 April. Their main aim was to capture the dozens of villages along the road from Jaffa to Jerusalem. For, although these villages lay outside the proposed Jewish state, the Haganah was determined to split the Arab state in two, to weaken its fighting power, and to capture Jerusalem before it came under UN control.

During the fighting for these villages, eighty soldiers of the Irgun killed the entire population of the village of Deir Yassin. Two hundred and fifty men, women and children were massacred in this suburb of Jerusalem, often after being tortured and mutilated. In all, nearly 200 Palestinian villages were attacked and occupied by Jewish forces before the end of the mandate on 15 May. Many villagers were killed in these attacks and most of the survivors fled from their home, never to return. As we shall see, this was the start of an appalling refugee problem that would cause conflict for many years to come.

Operation Dalet also involved the capture of several major towns that were meant to be part of the Arab state – Tiberias, Haifa and Jaffa. In Jerusalem itself, which was due to become an international zone run by the UN, the Haganah occupied most of the Arab areas of West Jerusalem.

On 15 May 1948 the British mandate ended and the Arab and Jewish states came into being. The Jews named their state Israel and formed a government led by David Ben Gurion. One day later, five neighbouring Arab countries sent armies to make war on Israel. The civil war was about to turn into an international war, the first of a series of Arab–Israeli conflicts that has rocked the Middle East since 1948.

B. *Arab inhabitants of Haifa driven out of the city by the Jewish attack in April 1948*

Work section

A. Study the map opposite:
1. Describe the problems likely to arise for both the Arab and Jewish states under the following headings: road and rail communications; seaborne trade; military defence; water power and water supply; size of state.
2. Judging by the map as well as by what you have read in this chapter, who do you think benefited most from the partition plan, Jews or Arabs? Explain your answer.

B. Study photographs A and B in this chapter. Then, in as much detail as possible, describe the ways in which the scenes in the two photographs are (a) similar to each other, and (b) different.

6

'LIBERATION' AND 'CATASTROPHE'

Israel's 'War of Liberation'

On 15 May 1948 armies from Egypt, Lebanon, Transjordan, Iraq and Syria entered Palestine. Their aim was to help the Palestinian Arabs fight the Jewish state of Israel which had been created that day.

Within three weeks the Syrians and Iraqis had driven deep into Israel. The Arab Legion of Transjordan had taken back control of the Old City of Jerusalem which the Israelis had occupied. A third of Israel was in Arab hands.

The Arabs could not follow up this early advantage. Their armies consisted of around 20,000 men fighting nearly 65,000 Israeli troops. They had no unified command and they lacked modern weapons. After the United Nations arranged a truce on 11 June, the Israelis reorganised their army and transported the Czech weapons they had bought earlier in the year from Europe (see page 10). So when the truce ended in July 1948 the Israelis were able to fight back with great force. In ten days they seized western Galilee and a large part of central Palestine before the United Nations could arrange another truce.

The second truce lasted until 15 October, when the Israelis attacked the Egyptians and swept them out of the Negev desert. At the end of October they attacked the Lebanese in the north and drove them back into Lebanon. By the end of 1948 the Arab armies had abandoned the struggle, leaving Israel in control of 80 per cent of the land area of Palestine. A series of armistice (ceasefire) agreements between the Arab states and Israel brought an end to the war and left Israel in possession of all that land.

Palestine's 'Year of Catastrophe'

Israelis call 1948 their 'Year of Liberation', but Palestinians remember it as their 'Year of Catastrophe'. For, during the fighting between the Arabs and Israelis, nearly a million Palestinians left or were forced to leave their homes. Most went to Jordan (as Transjordan was now called) and the Gaza Strip. The remainder went to Syria and Lebanon, where they settled in refugee camps such as the one in the photograph below. Few were able to return to Palestine and they remain today a homeless people, living in refugee camps in the Arab states.

Ever since 1948 Arabs and Israelis have argued about what caused this great exodus of Palestinians. Sources A to G have been chosen to illustrate the different explanations that have been put forward.

There is much evidence to suggest that the exodus began with the massacre at Deir Yassin in April 1948 (see page 11). Menachim Begin, leader of the Irgun which carried out the massacre, wrote in 1951:

A. 'Arabs throughout the country, induced to believe wild tales of 'Irgun butchery', were seized with limitless panic and started to flee for their lives. This mass flight soon developed into a maddened, uncontrollable stampede.'

A French Red Cross worker, Jacques de Reynier, who visited Deir Yassin the day after the massacre, wrote in 1950 that:

B. 'The affair of Deir Yassin had immense repercussions. The press and radio spread the news everywhere among Arabs as well as the Jews. In this way a general terror was built up among the Arabs. . . . Driven by fear, the Arabs left their homes to find shelter among their kindred; first isolated farms, then villages, and in the end whole towns were evacuated.'

According to many accounts, the panic caused by the Deir Yassin massacre spread all over Palestine. In Jerusalem, according to an Israeli writing in 1964:

C. 'An uncontrolled panic swept through all Arab quarters, the Israelis brought up jeeps with loudspeakers which broadcast recorded 'horror sounds'. These included shreiks, wails and anguished moans of Arab women, the wail of

A Palestinian refugee camp in Lebanon, 1952

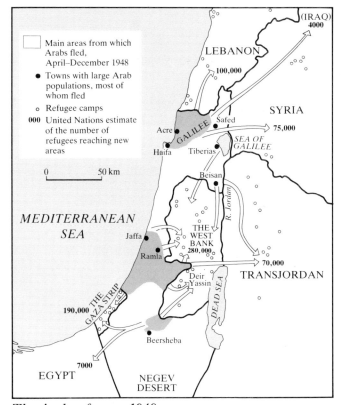

The Arab refugees, 1948

sirens and the clang of fire alarm bells, interrupted by a sepulchral voice calling out in Arabic "Save your souls, all ye faithful: the Jews are using poison gas and atomic weapons. Run for your lives in the name of Allah."'

Two Israeli journalists wrote in 1960 that:

D. '[On 11 July, Moshe Dayan and his troops] drove at full speed into Lidda shooting up the town and creating confusion and a degree of terror among the population. . . . Its Arab population of 30,000 either fled or were herded on the road to Ramallah. The next day Ramleh also surrendered and its Arab population suffered the same fate. Both towns were sacked by the victorious Israelis.'

Most Israelis give a different explanation of the Arab exodus. According to the Britain–Israel Public Affairs Committee, an Israeli information service:

E. 'If the Arabs were so attached to their land, why did they leave it during a crisis? The blame must be attributed to Arab leaders who, expecting a quick victory by their five combined armies over Israel, encouraged Arabs to leave Palestine, promising them that on their return they would be able to claim the property of the Jews as well. Arab propaganda led them to fear what would happen to them if they stayed, and threatened that they would also be considered traitors to the Arab cause.'

One source of evidence often used to support this point of view is a statement allegedly made in August 1948 by the Greek Catholic Archbishop of Galilee:

F. 'The refugees had been confident that their absence from Palestine would not last long; that they would return in a few days – within a week or two; their leaders had promised them that the Arab armies would crush the "Zionist gangs" very quickly and that there would be no need for panic or fear of a long exile.'

But according to Erskine Childers, an Irish journalist writing in 1961, the Archbishop's evidence is unreliable:

G. 'I wrote to His Grace, asking for his evidence of such orders. I hold signed letters, with permission to publish, in which he has categorically denied ever alleging Arab evacuation orders; he states that no such order were ever given. He says that his name has been abused for years, and that the Arabs fled through panic and forcible eviction by Jewish troops. . .

I next decided to test the . . . charge that the Arab evacuation orders were broadcast by Arab radio – which could be done thoroughly because the BBC monitored all Middle Eastern broadcasts throughout 1948. The records, and companion ones by a U.S. monitoring unit can be seen at the British Museum.

There was not a single order, or appeal, or suggestion about evacuation from Palestine from any Arab radio station, inside or outside Palestine in 1948. There is a repeated monitored record of Arab appeals, even flat orders, to the civilians of Palestine to stay put.'

While there is disagreement about what caused the exodus of Arabs from Palestine, there is no argument about its immediate results. As the map above shows, the Arab state of Palestine ceased to exist. Three quarters of a million Palestinians became refugees living in neighbouring states and the rest of the Palestinians remained in the new state of Israel as a minority people.

Work section

A. 1. Using sources A to D as evidence, list four causes of the Palestinian exodus of 1948.
2. What different causes are suggested in sources E to G?
3. How reliable do you consider each of sources A to D?
4. In what ways does source G disagree with the views in sources E and F?
5. How reliable do you consider source G?
6. In the light of your answers to questions 1 to 5, what do you think caused the exodus of 1948?

B. Using the map and photograph in this chapter, describe the consequences of the 1948 exodus.

Revision guide

You may find it helpful to make notes on what you have read so far. If you are not sure how to organise your notes, this list of headings and sub-headings shows the main points that should be noted.

A. The religious and historical background
1. Jews
2. Christians
3. Muslims

B. Zionism and Arab nationalism
1. The Jewish dispersion
2. Zionism
3. The Great War and Arab nationalism
   - The Hussein–McMahon letters
   - The Arab Revolt
   - The Sykes–Picot Agreement
4. The Balfour Declaration

C. The start of the conflict, 1919–36
1. The peace settlement in the Middle East
2. The British mandate in Palestine
3. Violence between Arabs and Jews
4. The 1936 General Strike

D. Challenges to British rule, 1937–47
1. The Peel Report, 1937
2. The Arab rebellion, 1937–39
3. The 1939 White Paper

4. Palestine and the Second World War
5. The Holocaust
6. Changing methods of the Zionists
   - The Biltmore Programme
   - 'Illegal' immigration
   - Terror tactics

E. The end of British rule, 1947–48
1. The United Nations partition plan
2. Palestinian objections to the plan
3. Civil war in Palestine
   - The Haganah
   - The Arab League
   - Operation Dalet
   - Deir Yassin
4. Proclamation of the State of Israel

F. 1948: 'Liberation' and 'Catastrophe'
1. Israel's 'War of Liberation'
   - Events and results
2. The exodus of Palestinians
   - Causes
   - Results

Revision exercise

The following passage is taken from an interview by a British journalist with old men in a Palestinian refugee camp in Lebanon. The interview was recorded in 1979. Read it carefully and then answer the questions which follow.

> You are British and we find it hard not to perceive the British as our enemy, because it was you who permitted our country to be stolen from us. But we make you welcome. At least you wish to hear. We will speak with you. . . .
>
> Put this in your book. The British cheated us. They promised us freedom and instead we had the Mandate. And do you know what the policy of the Mandate was? It said that we, the people of Palestine, were not mature enough to govern ourselves. That is what it meant. That we were not mature enough. And worse than that even, they brought ruin to our land and made us homeless; you, the British, brought foreigners to Palestine and made us exiles.'

A. Using information taken from Part One of this book, explain in your own words what the speaker meant by:
1. 'The British . . . promised us freedom.' (line 4)
2. '. . . the Mandate.' (line 5)
3. 'you, the British, brought foreigners to Palestine.' (line 8)
4. 'you . . . made us exiles.' (line 8)

B. Put yourself in the position of a British official in Palestine in the 1930s and reply to each of the above criticisms, defending Britain's rule in Palestine.

C. On what points might a Zionist have disagreed with the criticisms in the passage above *and* with the British reply to the criticisms you have given in exercise B?

PART TWO

THE CONFLICT

Jerusalem, 24 February 1948: Jews flee from the Jewish area after a bomb killed 51 people there. Haganah, blaming the British for the explosion, killed nine Britons in reprisal before Arabs claimed responsibility for it

Wars between countries usually end in two stages. The first is an armistice, or agreement to stop fighting. The second is a peace treaty, a permanent and binding settlement of the issues for which each side fought.

The 1948 war between Israel and the Arabs ended with a series of armistices, but not with a peace treaty. During 1949 Egypt, Lebanon, Jordan and Syria signed armistices with Israel, agreeing to a cease-fire until a final peace settlement could be made. But since then, only Egypt has signed a peace treaty with Israel. The rest remain Israel's bitter enemies. As the Secretary of the Arab League put it in 1949:

'As long as we don't make peace with the Zionists the war is not over. And as long as

the war is not over there is neither victor nor vanquished. As soon as we recognise the existence of Israel, we admit, by this act, that we are vanquished.'

In the eyes of most Arabs, there is no such country as Israel. The land occupied by Israel is still Palestine to them. Ever since the armistices of 1949, the Arab states surrounding Israel have talked about destroying it and of restoring the Arab state of Palestine.

This has led to four major wars between Israel and her Arab neighbours – in 1956, 1967, 1973 and 1982–85. The conflict between them is still as sharp today as it was in 1949. Part Two of this book looks closely at the causes and consequences of each of those wars, in an attempt to explain why the conflict has lasted so long and still shows no sign of ending.

15

7

UNEASY PEACE, 1949–1955

The new state of Israel

As you have read, the Zionists' aim in creating Israel was to give Jews a nation of their own. Their first priority in 1948 was, therefore, to take in Jews from all over the world and to make them citizens of Israel.

Jews started to flood into Israel as soon as it was created. The first to come were survivors of the Holocaust, existing in refugee camps in Germany, Italy and Austria. Next to arrive were Jewish communities from Eastern Europe, especially Poland and Romania.

Then came Jews from the Arab world. Around half a million Jews had lived in the Arab countries of Africa and the Middle East since ancient times. In 1948, however, they became the victims of persecution. Hundreds were killed in anti-Jewish riots. In Iraq, Zionism was made a crime punishable by death. Syria forced Jews to live in ghettoes. The result of this persecution was a flood of Jewish refugees from the Arab world, seeking refuge in Israel: 45,000 from the Yemen, 100,000 from Iraq, and 350,000 from the countries of North Africa.

In 1950 Israel's first law, the **Law of Return**, entitled any Jew to settle in Israel and to become an Israeli citizen. By the end of 1951, 687,000 Jewish immigrants had landed in Israel, bringing the population up to 1.5 million. This made the situation worse for the Palestinians who had fled in 1948. Most of the homes which they left empty were occupied by Jewish newcomers, who could find nowhere to live. And with more and more Jews arriving each year, it became less and less likely that Israel could ever allow all the Palestinians to return to their homes.

The growth of Israel's population after 1948 led to friction with neighbouring Arab states. With so many new people to feed, Israel had to create more farms and that meant increasing the supply of water for irrigation. When Israel started diverting the waters of the River Jordan towards dry farmland, the governments of Syria and Jordan protested angrily. Even when the United States government tried to ease the situation with a plan for sharing the water, the Arab states refused to discuss it – for to negotiate with Israel would be to admit that Israel existed.

Absorbing 687,000 Jews into Israel was expensive. Factories, farms, roads, railways, hospitals, schools and homes were all urgently needed. Israel therefore had to take aid from other countries, especially the USA, which gave $65 million to help Israel absorb Jewish immigrants. This confirmed the view of many Arabs that the USA was trying to gain influence in the Middle East by supporting Zionism.

Changes in the Arab world

The Arabs' defeat in 1948 led to many changes in the Arab world. The first was a change of leadership. Within ten years, nearly all the Arab governments of the Middle East were overthrown by violent means. In Egypt, the Prime Minister was assassinated in December 1948 following the defeat of Egyptian forces by Israel. In Syria, a series of military take-overs took place in 1949. In 1950 the Lebanese Prime Minister was assassinated. In 1951 King Abdullah of Jordan was murdered in Jerusalem. And in 1952 Egypt's King Farouk, a corrupt playboy, was overthrown by a group of army officers, led at first by General Neguib and later by Colonel Nasser.

A second change in the Arab world resulted from the political thinking of the new leaders who took power after 1948. Many of them blamed the defeat of 1948 on the British and Americans who, they said, had always helped the Zionists. This led to bad feeling towards Britain and the USA and to a belief that their influence in the Middle East must be

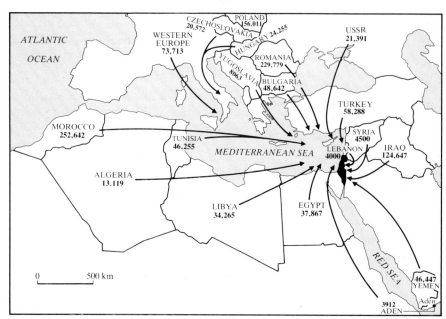

Jewish refugees, 15 May 1948–31 December 1967

Jews from Kurdistan arriving in Israel in 1951. Nearly the whole Jewish population of Kurdistan emigrated to Israel in 'Operation Ezra and Nehemiah' in 1951

destroyed. Instead, the Arab leaders believed the Middle East should be neutral in world affairs. Many of them also wanted to improve the economy and society of their countries – for example, by giving land to poor peasants and by improving public health and education. Finally, some of the new leaders hoped for a union of the Arab countries so that they could act together on matters of common interest.

There was, however, one matter of common interest – that of the Palestinian refugees – on which the Arab states took little action. With the exception of Jordan, they refused to give permanent homes to the refugees, nor would they allow them to become citizens of their countries. As a result, most Palestinians had to remain in their camps as stateless, unwelcome refugees.

The Fedayeen

In many refugee camps, young men known as **Fedayeen** (Arabic for 'self-sacrificers') formed commando groups to make guerilla attacks on Israel. Fedayeen secretly crossed the Israeli borders to attack lonely farms and frontier posts, to blow up pipelines and power stations, to mine roads and to machine-gun buses. Each year from 1949 to 1955 some 250 Israelis were killed or wounded in such attacks.

In reply to the Fedayeen attacks, the Israeli army made reprisal raids on the camps from which they came. But, unlike the attacks of the Fedayeen, these reprisals were military operations carried out by highly trained soldiers of the regular army. Often they used heavy guns, tanks and aircraft. Palestinian casualties after these raids were therefore usually high.

The cross-border conflict grew more serious each year. In 1953, after three Israelis were killed by a bomb, the Israeli army attacked the village of Qibya in Jordan destroying the whole village and killing sixty-six people. In 1955 the Israelis mounted a reprisal raid on the Gaza Strip after a series of Fedayeen attacks on their territory. In the Gaza raid, thirty-eight Egyptians were killed. And in a raid on Syria later in the year, the Israelis killed forty-nine Fedayeen.

Economic warfare

It wasn't only cross-border raids that made 1949–55 a time of uneasy peace. Tension was also caused by an Arab boycott of Israel's trade.

The boycott had started in 1946 when the Arab League called on its members not to buy goods made by Jews in Palestine. After Israel became a state in 1948, the Arab states tightened the boycott. Egypt stopped Israeli ships from using the Suez Canal. Ships bound for Israel calling at Arab ports had their cargoes confiscated. Israeli aircraft were not allowed to fly over Arab territory.

The boycott did not, as the Arabs hoped, destroy Israel's fragile economy. But, combined with the attacks of the Fedayeen, it kept Israel in a permanent state of tension.

Work section

A. Make sure you have understood pages 15 to 17 by explaining what the following words and terms mean: armistice; the Law of Return; Fedayeen; reprisal raids.

B. Study the photograph above and the map opposite, then answer these questions:
1. Using information from Chapters 1 and 2, explain why Jews lived in so many countries.
2. From which countries did Jews emigrate to Israel after 1948? What problems do you think Israel experienced as a result of (a) the different languages spoken by the immigrants, and (b) their different backgrounds?
3. Judging by what you have read so far, suggest why the people in the photograph seem happy?
4. In the light of your answer to question 2, what difficulties do you think the people in the photograph were likely to face in their new country?

THE SUEZ–SINAI WAR OF 1956

In 1956 a war began when Israel invaded Egypt. The war lasted only ten days and was an overwhelming victory for Israel. But this was more than an Arab–Israeli conflict, for the armed forces of France and Britain were also involved. The 1956 war thus had great international importance.

Causes of the war

The 1956 war had many causes. One was the behaviour of Egypt's new President, Gamal Abdel Nasser, the most able of the new Arab leaders who took power in the 1950s.

President Nasser wanted to avenge Egypt's defeat in the 1948 war against Israel and to return Palestine to the Arabs. He also hoped to unite the Arab states under Egypt's leadership. Both these aims needed an increase in Egypt's wealth and armed strength.

Nasser set about achieving his aims in a variety of ways. He persuaded the British to give up their military bases along the Suez Canal, thus increasing Egypt's independence. He gave aid to Arab rebels fighting the French in their colony of Algeria. He persuaded many Arab states not to join a British-backed military alliance called the Baghdad Pact, and instead formed an alliance between Egypt, Syria and Saudi Arabia. The armies of Egypt, Syria and Jordan were put under joint command. Nasser also persuaded King Hussein of Jordan to dismiss his British Chief of Staff, General Glubb, and to allow Fedayeen to attack Israel from Jordanian territory.

Nasser needed a modern, well-equipped army. In 1955 he made an arms agreement with Czechoslovakia to obtain fighter planes, bombers, warships, guns and tanks. Czechoslovakia was under the strong influence of the USSR and supplied the weapons under the orders of the USSR, which was involved in a 'Cold War' against the USA, Britain and their allies. The British and Americans saw this as a Soviet attempt to gain influence in the Middle East and thus improve its position in the Cold War. For this reason the British and Americans cancelled loans they had promised to Nasser for building a dam at Aswan on the River Nile.

The Aswan Dam was Nasser's most important project. He intended the dam to transform Egypt's economy by providing water for vast areas of new farmland, by generating electricity for new factories and by making the Nile navigable as far south as Sudan. It was to cost $1,400 million, of which Britain and the USA had promised $70 million.

When Britain and the USA cancelled the loans they had promised, Nasser nationalised the Suez Canal

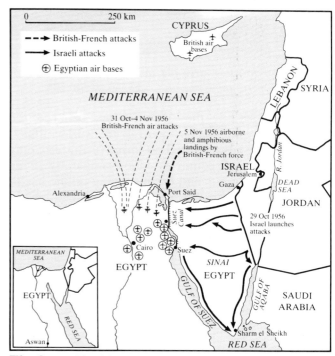

The Suez–Sinai War

Company, which was owned largely by British and French shareholders. His aim was to use the tolls paid by ships using the canal to pay for the Aswan Dam. Although Nasser promised to compensate shareholders, the British Prime Minister, Sir Anthony Eden, did not trust him. In a letter to the US President in September 1958, Eden wrote:

A. '. . . the seizure of the Suez Canal is, we are convinced, the opening gambit in a planned campaign designed by Nasser to expel all Western influence and interests from Arab countries. He believes that if he can get away with this, and if he can successfully defy eighteen nations, his prestige in Arabia will be so great that he will be able to mount revolutions of young officers in Saudi Arabia, Jordan, Syria and Iraq. . . .

These new governments will in effect be Egyptian satellites if not Russian ones. They will have to place their united oil resources under the control of a united Arabia led by Egypt and under Russian influence. When that moment comes Nasser can deny oil to Western Europe and we shall all be at his mercy.'

The French, angry about Nasser's support for the Arabs fighting them in Algeria, agreed with Eden. To weaken Nasser's growing power in the Middle East, Britain and France decided on a military invasion of the Suez Canal zone.

Meanwhile, the Fedayeen in Egypt and Jordan continued to make cross-border attacks on Israel. By 1956 their attacks were more daring and more violent than ever before. They were also managing to kill many of the Israeli soldiers who came after them in reprisal raids. To make matters worse, Egypt had closed the entrance of the Gulf of Aqaba to Israeli ships, cutting off Israel's only access to the Red Sea. Israel's leaders therefore planned a full-scale military invasion of Egypt to destroy the Fedayeen, to weaken Nasser, and to reopen the Gulf of Aqaba to Israeli ships. In October 1956 the Israeli leaders came together with the French and British. At a series of secret meetings in Paris, they agreed to make a joint attack on Egypt before the end of the month. France also agreed to supply Israel with arms, especially fighter aircraft which it lacked.

The Suez–Sinai War

The war began according to the plan agreed in Paris. Israel invaded Egypt on 29 October and advanced deep into Sinai. The next day, France and Britain ordered both Israel and Egypt to withdraw from the Suez Canal Zone, which was inside Egypt. When Egypt refused, the British and French bombed Egyptian airfields and landed troops at Port Said, saying that they were doing so to protect lives and shipping there. By that time (5 November) the Israelis had occupied all of Sinai.

The British-French attack on Egypt was greeted with loud and angry protests from all over the world. The United Nations voted for an immediate ceasefire. The Arab countries stopped supplying Britain with oil. In Britain itself, many people opposed their government's action. Most serious of all, the United States government refused to support the invasion. This quickly put Britain into an impossible

situation, for when the Arabs stopped its oil supplies, Britain had to ask the Americans for oil; and President Eisenhower refused to supply it until Britain and France had called a halt to their invasion.

Prime Minister Eden had no choice but to agree to a ceasefire, only 24 hours after the first British troops had landed in Egypt. While French and British troops left the Canal zone, a United Nations Emergency Force moved in to police the border between Egypt and Israel.

Results of the war

The war had important results for all the countries involved. For Israel, the war was a victory: 170 Israeli soldiers were killed, compared with 1000 Egyptian dead. The Israeli army had destroyed the bases of the Fedayeen, occupied all Sinai and reopened the Gulf of Aqaba to Israeli ships. Even when Israel withdrew from Sinai in 1957 the two most sensitive areas, Gaza and Sharm el-Sheikh, were taken over by UN forces, giving Israel protection against future attack.

The war was a disaster for both France and Britain. They had to leave Egypt without achieving a single one of their aims. They failed to overthrow President Nasser. They failed to keep the Suez Canal open, for Egypt blocked it by sinking ships in the middle of the Canal. They had to introduce petrol rationing as a result of the Arab ban on their oil supplies.

In the long run, the war strengthened the Arab states, even though Egypt had been defeated. Nasser's reputation as leader of the Arab world increased, while pro-Western governments in Jordan, Iraq and Lebanon turned against Britain and France. It seemed that Eden's worst fears were about to come true: a united Arab world under Nasser's control and influenced by the USSR.

Work section

A. This is a list of some *causes* and *results* of the 1956 Suez–Sinai War:
  - Egypt's military power was reduced
  - The Fedayeen made many attacks on Israel
  - Britain and France were humiliated
  - Britain and the USA cancelled loans for building the Aswan Dam
  - Nasser aimed to unite the Arab states under Egyptian leadership
  - Israel gained security against Fedayeen attacks
  - The 1955 arms agreement with Czechoslovakia gave Egypt many Soviet weapons
  - British influence in the Middle East declined
  - Nasser's reputation in the Arab world increased
  - Nasser nationalised the Suez Canal Company
  - Prime Minister Eden of Britain feared Nasser's intentions
  1. Find six causes of the 1956 Suez–Sinai war in the list above.
  2. Which of those causes do you consider the most important? Explain your answer.
  3. Find five results of the war in the list above.
  4. Which of those results do you consider the most important? Explain your answer.

B. Study source A, then answer these questions:
  1. In your own words, give four reasons why Eden feared Nasser's intentions.
  2. Reply to Eden's fears by explaining Nasser's behaviour as if you were a supporter of Nasser.

9

THE RESHAPING OF THE MIDDLE EAST, 1956–1967

In the ten years after 1956 the countries of the Middle East went through many important changes. Sadly, these changes kept the region in a state of tension and hostility. The result was a third war between Israel and the Arab countries in 1967.

The reshaping of the Arab world

In 1958 Iraq's pro-Western government was overthrown. In a military take-over King Feisal and his family were murdered, while Prime Minister Nuri Said was torn to pieces by a mob. The government which replaced them made Iraq an ally of both Egypt and the USSR.

The revolution in Iraq alarmed the Americans and the British who already feared the spread of Soviet influence in the Middle East. For this reason, British troops went to Jordan in 1958 to prevent revolutionaries from deposing King Hussein. In the same year, American marines went to Lebanon to prevent its government from being overthrown in a civil war. As a result of the British and American actions, Jordan and Lebanon kept their pro-Western governments.

Elsewhere in the Middle East, anti-Western attitudes continued to spread. In Egypt, President Nasser still aimed to unite the Arab world under his leadership and to build up the country's strength. From 1956 to 1959 he dominated the affairs of the Middle East and was very popular in Egypt, where he gave land to peasants, built new factories and continued work on the Aswan Dam. In 1958 his dream of Arab unity took another step towards reality when Syria and Egypt joined together in a **United Arab Republic**. The UAR was intended to be the foundation stone for an eventual union of all the Arab states.

In the early 1960s the move towards Arab unity ground to a halt. Syria, after another military take-over of its government, left the UAR in 1961 and started to quarrel with both Egypt and Iraq. The pro-Western king of Jordan quarrelled with both Syria and Egypt. Saudi Arabia and Egypt quarrelled with each other when they backed rival sides fighting a civil war in Yemen. Algeria fought with Morocco and Morocco had a dispute with Tunisia. The 1960s thus became a time of strife and disunity in the Arab world.

The reshaping of the Palestinians

The Palestinian Arabs, who were mostly still living in refugee camps in Lebanon, Jordan and Egypt, were bitterly disappointed by the failure of the Arab states to unite. They had hoped for a united Arab nation which would destroy Israel and allow them to return to their homes in Palestine.

With the failure of the UAR in 1961, hundreds of young Palestinians formed into secret resistance groups to work for a return to Palestine. They put out propaganda in magazines and posters, raised funds, recruited members, raided Israel's borders, and made contacts with revolutionaries in Vietnam and Cuba.

A. *A street in a Palestinian refugee camp in 1966*

In 1964 the Arab League brought these resistance groups together into a single body called the **Palestine Liberation Organisation**. At first, its campaign to liberate Palestine from Israeli rule was carried on mainly through propaganda. Some members disagreed with this. They believed they would have to fight with weapons rather than words to get back their land. They formed fighting groups and prepared for a guerilla war against Israel. Typical of these groups was the **Palestine National Liberation Movement**, known by its Arab initials in reverse as **Fatah**, which means 'Conquest'.

Fatah made its first guerilla attack on Israel in 1965. It soon became clear that Fatah was more effective and dangerous than the Fedayeen had been in the 1950s. As well as attacking targets close to the borders, Fatah probed deep into Israel, exploding bombs in Tel Aviv, blowing up railways, and killing civilians.

At first, most of the Arab countries mistrusted Fatah and its campaign of violence. They feared that Israel would make reprisal raids on any country sheltering Fatah members. So, in Jordan, King Hussein ordered his army to hunt down the guerillas. In Lebanon the police tortured guerillas to extract secrets from them. Only Syria, where the left-wing **Baath** (meaning 'Resurgence') Arab socialist party took power in 1963, gave support to Fatah, providing weapons, training facilities and bases from which to attack Israel. Syria also mounted big guns in the Golan Heights (see map on page 23) to shell Israeli villages across the border.

Israel replied to Fatah's attacks with reprisal raids, in great force and in daylight, by regular army units. But because it was difficult to attack Syria across the heavily-armed border in the Golan Heights, Israel's reprisals were mostly against Jordan. In a raid on the village of Samu in 1966, eighteen Jordanians were killed and much of the village was destroyed. During the raid, the Israelis also fought a battle with the Jordan Arab Legion. As a result, King Hussein of Jordan began to take a tougher attitude towards Israel. In the same month, Egypt and Syria signed a defence pact, agreeing to help each other in any future war.

The reshaping of Israel

For several years after the 1956 war, Israel enjoyed peace and security. The cross-border attacks of the Fedayeen had mostly ceased now that their bases in Egypt and Gaza had been destroyed. Israel was thus able to build up its strength. The population grew in ten years from 1,900,000 to 2,500,000. The area of farm land rapidly increased as new settlers cultivated desert areas. Many new factories opened and standards of living rose.

During the decade after 1956, Israel's standing in the world grew, for as time went by, other countries came to accept Israel as a permanent member of the world community. France became a firm ally, while Britain, France and the USA promised in 1957 that they would, if ever it was necessary, take action to keep the Gulf of Aqaba open to Israeli ships.

Israel did not escape problems during these years. An economic recession at the end of the 1950s led to unemployment: by 1967 some 100,000 workers had no jobs. Socially, gaps started to open up among the people of Israel – for example, between those who had come from Europe and those from Africa and the Middle East. The latter increasingly found they were discriminated against in jobs, housing and political life. On the whole, however, by 1967 Israel was stronger, richer and more stable than at any time since becoming independent in 1948.

B. *Dizengoff Street in Tel Aviv, then the capital of Israel, in 1966*

Work section

A. Check your knowledge and understanding of this chapter by explaining what the following words and terms mean: United Arab Republic; Palestine Liberation Organisation; Fatah; Baath Party.

B. Study photographs A and B carefully, then answer these questions:
1. In what ways does photograph B show that Israel had become prosperous in the twenty years after independence?
2. In what ways do the living conditions of the Palestinians in photograph A appear different to those in photograph B?
3. Compare photograph A with the photograph on page 12. In what ways do the conditions of the Palestinians appear to have changed between 1952 and 1966?
4. How reliable do you consider photographs A and B as evidence of the living conditions of Israelis and Palestinian refugees? Explain your answer.

THE SIX DAY WAR OF 1967

A cartoon in a Lebanese newspaper on 31 May 1967 shows Israel facing the armed forces of eight Arab states

In June 1967 Israel went to war again with the Arab states around it. This time the Arabs were well armed and well prepared. It seemed certain that Israel would be beaten.

The road to war

The road to this war began in Syria, where the army again overthrew the government in 1966. General Jedid, Syria's new leader after the take-over, gave important government posts to the extreme left-wing Baath Party. With extremists now in control of both the army and the government, Syria became violently anti-Israel. Attacks by Fatah guerillas from Syria increased. Large numbers of Syrian troops were stationed in the Golan Heights, on Israel's border. The Syrian radio and press mounted a propaganda campaign of hate against Israel.

Tension between Syria and Israel grew in spring 1967 when Israeli farmers started cultivating land close to the border. When an Israeli tractor ploughed up some Arab-owned land there on 7 April, Syrian troops opened fire on it. In reply the Israeli air force bombed the Syrian guns and shot down six Syrian fighter planes sent to attack them.

The Syrians continued to attack Israel even after this defeat and so, on 11 May, Israel's Prime Minister Eshkol warned that Israel would strike back hard if the attacks went on. Israel's military leader said that Israeli forces might attack Damascus, Syria's capital.

At this point the government of the USSR involved itself in the dispute. The USSR was Syria's ally, supplying it with money, weapons and training. On 12 May the USSR told Syria and Egypt that Israel was massing its armed forces on the Syrian border, ready to invade Syria in one week's time.

This was not true. The USSR was either misinformed or lying. Nevertheless the story quickly spread throughout the Arab countries and was widely believed. King Feisal of Saudi Arabia and King Hussein of Jordan promised to help defend Syria. President Nasser put Egypt's armed forces on alert and moved 100,000 troops to Sinai.

On 16 May Nasser increased the tension by ordering the United Nations Emergency Force, which had been patrolling the border between Israel and Egypt since 1956, to leave Egyptian territory. The UN Secretary-General, U Thant, realised that the UN force was too small to prevent a war between Egypt and Israel and ordered it to withdraw.

On 23 May Nasser took the even more extreme step of barring the Gulf of Aqaba to Israeli ships. As in 1956, this made war between Israel and Egypt a virtual certainty.

The Arab world was delighted by Nasser's actions. Arabs talked openly of wiping out the state of Israel in the coming war. The Syrian Minister of Defence, for example, said on 24 May:

A. 'We shall never call for, nor accept peace. We shall only accept war. . . . We have resolved to drench this land with your blood, to oust you, aggressors, and throw you into the sea for good.'

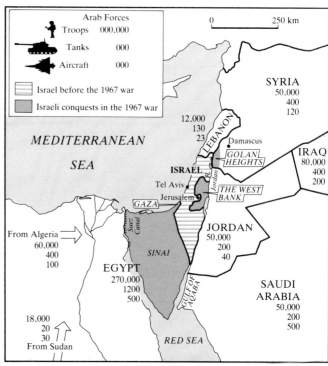

The Six Day War, 5–10 June 1967

On 28 May Jordan and Egypt formed a defence pact and put their armed forces under joint command. Iraq joined the pact a day later. Syria, as you have read, already had a pact with Egypt. By the start of 1967, Israel's chances of survival seemed remote. Eight Arab states were poised to attack. Egypt had 100,000 men and 1000 tanks in Sinai. On Egypt's airfields there were 400 fighter planes and 80 bombers, many only twelve minutes flying time from Tel Aviv. Lebanon, Syria, Jordan, Iraq, Saudi Arabia, Sudan and Algeria had 320,000 men and 1000 aircraft ready to strike across Israel's other borders.

Faced with this massive threat, the Israeli government reorganised itself into a 'Government of National Unity' in which all political parties had a place. The key post in the new government, that of Minister of Defence, was taken by a soldier, General Moshe Dayan. On his advice, the new government decided that the best form of defence was attack; in other words, to attack the Arabs before they could attack Israel, in the hope of taking them by surprise.

The Six Day War

War began on 5 June 1967 and lasted six days. In fact, its outcome was decided in only one day, the first.

At breakfast time on Monday 5 June, all but twelve planes of the Israeli airforce took off with orders to bomb Egypt's airfields. By 11 o'clock they had bombed all the airfields, destroying around 300 aircraft while they were still on the ground. Later in the day the Israelis launched similar attacks against the other Arab air forces. By nightfall, almost the whole of the Syrian and Jordanian air forces had been destroyed. Israel had control of the skies of the Middle East.

After 5 June, Israel was able to concentrate on fighting the war on land. Israeli troops moved with amazing speed against the Egyptians, driving them out of the Gaza Strip and Sinai, all the way back to the Suez Canal. Egypt's defeat was total. Some 3000 men were killed, 800 tanks and thousands of other vehicles were destroyed.

Israel defeated Jordan within two days, capturing the old city of Jerusalem and occupying all Jordan west of the Jordan river (the 'West Bank'). Finally, the Israelis attacked the Syrian army in the heavily fortified Golan Heights, seizing the whole area by 10 June. On that day the United Nations ordered a cease-fire. The Arabs had no choice but to accept it, for they no longer had the means to fight.

The results of the war

The war had important results for the whole of the Middle East. After the war, Israel was much safer and stronger than before. Ignoring a UN order to return captured territory, the Israelis kept Sinai, the Gaza Strip, the West Bank and the Golan Heights. This doubled the size of the country and also made its frontiers shorter and therefore easier to defend.

For the Arabs the war was a total disaster. In six days 15,000 of their men had been killed and 430 of their aircraft and 800 of their tanks had been captured or destroyed. They had lost nearly 70,000 km^2 of land. Their pride and prestige had been crushed.

The war brought more suffering to the Palestinians. A million Palestinians who had been living in the West Bank and the Gaza Strip suddenly found themselves in 'Occupied Territories', under Israeli rule. Around 250,000 of them fled across the Jordan river, adding to the already huge population of refugees living in Jordan. For many of those who stayed, Israeli rule meant restrictions on their lives such as travel and work permits, and heavy police surveillance. Thousands, suspected of being security risks, had their homes destroyed by Israeli troops.

Finally, Palestinians everywhere lost faith in the ability of the Arab states to defeat Israel and give them back their homeland. Increasingly after the Six Day War they put their trust in the only organisation that held out hope of liberating Palestine – Fatah.

Work section

A. Refer back to Chapter 8 on the 1956 Suez–Sinai War. Using the following headings, show in two columns (a) similarities between the 1956 and 1967 wars, and (b) differences between the two wars.
- Involvement of major world powers
- Behaviour of President Nasser
- Countries which fought against Israel
- Role played by the United Nations
- Duration of the wars
- Methods of warfare
- Results of the wars

Example:	Similarities	Differences
Involvement of major world powers	USSR backed Arabs in both wars	Britain and France involved in 1956 war but not in 1967
Behaviour of President Nasser	. . . .	. . . .

B. Study the cartoon opposite, then answer the following questions:
1. Explain the point made by the cartoon.
2. Judging by this chapter, what evidence did the cartoonist have for this point of view?
3. How was Israel able to get out of the situation shown in the cartoon?

11

WAR BY OTHER MEANS, 1967–1973

Israel's victory in the Six Day War did not bring peace to the Middle East. From 1967 to 1973 the Arabs continued their struggle with Israel, using means other than full-scale war.

Diplomacy

The first of those means was by diplomacy – that is, negotiation with other countries. In the United Nations the Arab states and their ally, the USSR, tried to cancel Israel's gains in the Six Day War by proposing that Israel must withdraw from all the conquered territory. Most countries in the UN, however, felt that Israel had been the victim of Arab aggression and voted against the proposal.

In November 1967 the UN Security Council drew up a new proposal for ending the Arab–Israeli conflict. **Resolution 242**, as the Security Council's proposal was called, said that Israel should withdraw from the occupied territories. It suggested a peace settlement in which the Arabs would recognise Israel's right to exist, and said that the Palestinian refugees must have fair treatment.

Egypt and Jordan accepted Resolution 242, while Syria rejected it. Israel, while accepting it, said it could not be a substitute for a specific agreement. Resolution 242 therefore failed to bring peace to the Middle East.

The war of attrition

Despite being shattered in the Six Day War, Egypt quickly regained the means to fight, for the USSR supplied large numbers of new weapons to replace those lost in the war. Hundreds of Soviet advisers helped to retrain and reorganise the armed forces.

Fighting between Egypt and Israel therefore began again in 1968. Egyptian guns shelled Israeli ships in the Gulf of Suez. In reply, Israeli guns bombarded Egyptian cities on the other side of the Suez Canal. When Egyptian missiles then sank an Israeli warship, Israeli guns bombarded oil refineries around Suez.

In 1969 President Nasser of Egypt announced a 'war of attrition' against Israel. This meant that Egypt's armed forces would make frequent small-scale attacks on Israel's border defences, hoping to wear them down. Israel replied by making commando raids on bridges and towns in the Nile Valley and by bombing Egyptian cities.

To protect Egypt from these raids, the USSR provided new and deadly weapons such as the SAM-3 missile, which could defend important targets like the Aswan Dam. A hundred fighter aircraft and eighty missile bases manned by 20,000 Soviet troops were installed on Egyptian soil. This forced Israel to give up its attacks on Egypt.

By 1970 both Israel and Egypt realised that neither of them could win the war of attrition and in that year they agreed to a ceasefire.

The guerilla war

Meanwhile the Palestinians were fighting their own war against Israel. In the months after the Six Day War, Fatah recruited many new members among the Palestinians of the West Bank who were now under Israeli rule. Fatah also collected large numbers of weapons left behind by the Arabs on the battlefields of the Six Day War. With this new stock of arms, Fatah was able to make more and more guerilla attacks on Israel, killing ninety-seven Israeli soldiers by the end of 1967.

The Israelis responded with harsh reprisals. Its strongest reprisal came on 21 March 1968 when 1500 Israeli troops, backed by tanks and aircraft, crossed the River Jordan and chased Fatah guerillas to their headquarters in the refugee town of Karameh. The Jordanian army treated this as an invasion of their country and fought the Israelis as they crossed the river. By the time the Israelis got to Karameh, the Fatah guerillas were waiting for them. In a long battle in which the town was destroyed, 40 Jordanian soldiers, 200 Palestinians and 28 Israelis were killed. Despite their losses, Fatah saw the Battle of Karameh as a heroic day in their struggle against Israel. Throughout the Arab world the dead Palestinians were treated as martyrs. From then on, Fatah was recognised as the leading force in the struggle to liberate Palestine.

Fatah grew stronger after the Battle of Karameh. By 1970 the organisation had some 30,000 fighters. Yassir Arafat, leader of Fatah, became Chairman of the PLO, and was soon an important figure in the Arab world. Fatah raids on Israel rose to an average of one a day by 1970. Between 1967 and 1970 Fatah guerillas killed 543 Israeli soldiers and 116 civilians, more than Israel had lost in the Six Day War.

King Hussein of Jordan, where most of the Palestinian refugees now lived, disliked Fatah and the PLO, for they were a threat to his authority. In Jordan's towns, for example, Fatah men displayed their strength by driving around in jeeps bristling with weapons, organising roadblocks to question passers-by, and forcing the public to give money to their cause.

Tension between King Hussein and the PLO rose as new guerilla groups, using extreme methods, came into being. The most important of these was the

A. *Airliners being blown up by the PFLP at Dawson's Field in Jordan, in September 1970*

Popular Front for the Liberation of Palestine (PFLP) led by Dr George Habash. The PFLP became well known when it organised a series of aircraft hijacks in which many civilians died. Dr Habash described the aim of the hijacks:

B. 'When we hijack a plane it has more effect than if we killed a hundred Israelis in battle. For decades world public opinion has been neither for nor against the Palestinians. It simply ignored us. At least the world is talking about us now.'

The PFLP's most spectacular hijack took place in 1970 when they forced three airliners to land at Dawson's Field, an airstrip in Jordan, and blew them up before hundreds of news cameramen who had rushed from all over the world to report the event.

The Dawson's Field hijackings provoked King Hussein into action. In September 1970 he ordered his army to expel the PLO from Jordan. During 'Black September', as the PLO called that month, the Jordanian army killed many guerillas and forced the PLO to retreat into Syria and Lebanon, where it set up new headquarters in Beirut, capital of Lebanon.

Although Hussein succeeded in driving the PLO out of Jordan, he could not stop small groups from carrying out a campaign of terror. In 1971 the PFLP and a new group called the **Black September Organisation** assassinated the Prime Minister of Jordan. Their most sensational act took place in 1972 when they kidnapped eleven Israeli athletes taking part in the Olympic Games in Munich. In a gun-fight with West German police, all the athletes as well as five of the Palestinians were killed.

Many people outside the Middle East condemned such actions. The West German President, speaking at the funeral service of the athletes, said:

C. 'Who is responsible for this black deed? In the forefront is a criminal organisation which believes in hatred and murder as political weapons.'

How did the 'terrorists', as the Western press now called the PLO fighters, explain their actions? One example of an explanation was given by a Palestinian teenager, speaking to a British journalist in 1978:

D. 'We are not terrorists. We do not bomb women and children. The world should know this. We are against Israel and imperialism. Nor are we against the Jews. We do not understand anti-semitism. That is European. We want our land back. When a commando goes into Israel he puts a bomb into a place defended by Israelis; he attacks offices and public places which are the centres of imperialism. The bombs are for the soldiers. If we place a bomb in a bus, it is a bus carrying soldiers, a military target. They are not civilians. If women and children are killed it is by mistake and we regret it, but we have no alternative.'

Work section

A. Check your understanding of this chapter by explaining the following words and terms: Resolution 242; war of attrition; Popular Front for the Liberation of Palestine; the Black September Organisation; terrorists.

B. Study sources A to D, then answer the following questions:
  1. According to source B, what was the aim of the PFLP in hijacking aircraft?
  2. Why do you think the PFLP blew up the aircraft in source A?
  3. Suggest why source A appeared in most of the world's newspapers the day after the photograph was taken. How far does this confirm the opinion expressed in source B?
  4. Explain the difference between being 'against Israel' and 'against the Jews' as the speaker in Source D sees it.
  5. From what you have read so far do you find any part of Source D hard to believe? Give your reasons.

YOM KIPPUR TO CAMP DAVID

Los Angeles Times

LARGEST CIRCULATION IN THE WEST, 1,020,987 DAILY, 1,309,677 SUNDAY

VOL. XCVI   SIX PARTS—PART ONE   112 PAGES   MONDAY MORNING, NOVEMBER 21, 1977   CC †   Copyright © 1977 Los Angeles Times   DAILY 15c

SADAT ACCEPTS ISRAEL AS A NATION
Begin Opens Borders to Egypt; but Deadlock Remains

PROS, CONS
Equal Rights Amendment: Is It Needed?

BY PHILIP HAGER
Times Staff Writer

WASHINGTON—True or false: Under the Equal Rights Amendment, women would be subject to the draft, separate public schools for boys and girls would be abolished and men would have the same right to alimony as women.

The answer: True, according to most legal authorities.

True or false: Under the amendment, prohibitions on homosexual marriage would be overturned, unisex public restrooms would be mandated and separate college dormitories for men and women would be prohibited.

The answer to all these questions is False, according to the same authorities.

But confident as authorities are on these questions, based largely on the stated intent of Congress in approving the amendment, confusion and uncertainty still surround the ERA, and authorities concede that nobody can

TALK OF PEACE—Egyptian President Anwar Sadat delivers historic address to Knesset in Jerusalem at left. At right, Israeli Prime Minister Menahem Begin gestures while giving his reply as Sadat listens at his side. Sadat said he made trip at "great risk."

2 Leaders Firm on Key Differences

BY DIAL TORGERSON
Times Staff Writer

JERUSALEM—Only slight cracks appeared Sunday in the stone-wall deadlock between Egypt and Israel as Anwar Sadat and Menahem Begin debated war and peace before the Israeli Knesset and the world.

In his historic speech to the country's lawmakers, the Egyptian president offered Israel firm recognition as a Middle East state, something he has never done in such a public forum.

In his reply, the Israeli prime minister said he was opening his borders to Egypt and called for meetings between Israel and the Arab confrontation states prior to a Geneva peace conference—a position similar to that of Egypt and one that could expedite the move toward Geneva.

But hopes that a dramatic breakthrough would be announced were

Text of Sadat and Begin speeches, Part 1, Pages 20 and 21. Related stories on Pages 18, 22 and 24.

dashed when Sadat and Begin spoke. Basically, the positions spelled out by the two leaders followed the line each side has held at Geneva peace talks seemed to be pending.

The Sadat initiative of 1977, as reported by a leading US newspaper

In September 1970 President Nasser of Egypt died. His place was taken by Anwar Sadat whose main aim was to reverse the Arab defeat of 1967 by pushing Israel out of Sinai, the West Bank and the Golan Heights. As this would almost certainly involve another war with Israel, Sadat asked the USSR for more weapons, especially fighter planes, missiles and tanks.

By 1973 Egypt was ready for war. Plans were made for an invasion of Sinai across the Suez Canal. Syria, which also received huge quantities of Soviet weapons, agreed to attack the Golan Heights at the same time as Egypt attacked Sinai – Saturday, 6 October 1973.

The Yom Kippur War

The Egyptians and Syrians chose 6 October because it was, in Israel, the Day of Atonement – *Yom Kippur* in Hebrew – when Jews ask God to forgive their sins. As this was the holiest day of prayer in the Jewish calendar, Israel's defences would be undermanned, with many soldiers on leave.

At 2 p.m. on 6 October the Egyptian and Syrian invasion began according to plan. Egyptian guns smashed Israel's Suez Canal defences with a bombardment of 175 shells per second. Thousands of commandos crossed the Canal in rubber dinghies and seized many Israeli fortresses. Engineers quickly built pontoon bridges over the water. By nightfall, 80,000 Egyptians had crossed the Canal. Israeli tanks which raced in to attack them were met with a hail of rocket fire that destroyed two thirds of them. In the north, the Syrian army with 1000 tanks advanced into the Golan Heights and drove the Israelis back into Galilee. Israel seemed on the brink of defeat.

Although the Israelis were taken by surprise on Yom Kippur, the fact that it was a holiday helped them recover. Most of Israel's 254,000 reserve soldiers were at home that day, and were quickly contacted with orders telling them to report for duty. And because Israel's roads and railways were empty, men, lorries, tanks and guns could be moved quickly to the battle areas. Helped by the United States government, which rushed $2200 million worth of the latest weapons to Israel, they were able to halt the Syrians in the north. The USSR, not to be outdone, airlifted huge stocks of weapons to Syria and Egypt, allowing them to mount new attacks on Israel.

With both Arabs and Israelis being equipped by the 'superpowers', the fighting between them was on a very big scale. On 14 October Egyptian and Israeli forces fought a massive tank battle in Sinai. It was the largest tank battle of the twentieth century and, by its end, the Egyptians had lost 250 tanks, against only ten Israeli losses.

Their victory in Sinai allowed the Israelis to cross the Suez Canal into Egypt, encircling the Egyptian 3rd Army. The USSR saw this happening in photographs taken by a space satellite, and advised President Sadat to agree to a ceasefire. The Soviets warned him that Egypt risked total defeat if the war went on.

Both the superpowers, the USA and the USSR, wanted an end to the Yom Kippur war, even though they had made it possible by supplying each side with weapons. The Soviets wanted it to stop because they could see that the Egyptians, whom they backed, would lose if they went on fighting. The Americans wanted it to end because they feared that any further Israeli attacks would provoke the Soviets into giving even more weapons to Egypt and Syria.

In the United Nations the USA and the USSR therefore jointly proposed a ceasefire. Egypt and Israel agreed to it and it came into force on 22 October. Within a day, however, a new crisis developed; Israel broke the ceasefire in order to finish encircling the Egyptian 3rd Army. This alarmed the USSR who feared the total defeat of Egypt. When the USSR suggested sending airborne troops to help Egypt, the President of the USA put the American armed forces on nuclear alert – their last stage of preparation for war. Although the USSR promptly dropped its suggestion and the nuclear alert was soon over, the incident showed how closely the superpowers were involved in the Arab-Israeli conflict.

Results of the war

Israel claimed victory in the Yom Kippur war: 12,000 Arabs had been killed, against 2000 Israelis; Israel had survived a surprise attack on two fronts and had captured even more territory from Syria and Egypt.

The war had important results for the rest of the world, chiefly because the Arab countries used their so-called **Oil Weapon**. During the war the Organisation of Arab Petroleum Exporting Countries (OAPEC) increased the price of Arab oil by 70 per cent and decided to reduce oil production by 5 per cent each month until Israel withdrew from Egypt and Syria. Saudi Arabia also imposed a total ban on oil shipments to the USA and the Netherlands (the main distribution point for European oil), whom they claimed were pro-Israeli. In December 1973 the OAPEC countries raised their prices again, this time by 128 per cent. This meant that oil prices had risen fourfold in under a year. The result was an economic crisis in countries which depended on foreign oil. In such countries, economic growth stopped, money lost its value through inflation, and millions of people lost their jobs.

Hoping to prevent the Arab 'oil weapon' from doing any more damage, the USA and its allies worked hard to appease the Arabs. Britain stopped supplying arms to Israel. The EEC expressed sympathy for Palestinians. Japan stopped supporting Israel. The US Secretary of State, Henry Kissinger, went to the Middle East and arranged a 'disengagement' of Israeli and Egyptian forces in January 1974.

The disengagement of forces meant that both sides drew back from their ceasefire positions, and the area between them was occupied by a United Nations army. In 1975 Kissinger brought about a further agreement by which Israel withdrew from parts of western Sinai and in return got more American aid.

Sadat's initiative and Camp David

In 1977 President Sadat surprised the world by going to Israel and speaking to Israel's parliament, the *Knesset*, about the terms on which Egypt would make peace. Sadat's visit was important for two reasons. First, the very fact that he was in Israel showed that Egypt now recognised Israel's existence. Second, the visit led to peace talks between Egypt and Israel during the next two years. The most important of these took place at **Camp David**, the US President's holiday retreat in Maryland, USA.

At Camp David in September 1978 the Israeli Prime Minister, Menachim Begin, talked about peace with President Sadat under the chairmanship of President Carter of the USA. They agreed that Israel would gradually leave Sinai and go back to the borders of 1948. Israel agreed to allow Palestinians in the West Bank some rights of self government within five years. Egypt agreed to allow ships going to and from Israel to use the Suez Canal.

The Camp David Agreement was confirmed by a treaty signed in Washington in 1979. After thirty years of conflict, Egypt and Israel were at peace with each other. This, however, caused fury in the Arab world. The PLO, as well as the Syrian, Libyan and Algerian governments, publicly condemned Sadat's action. And, on 6 October 1981, angry Egyptian soldiers murdered President Sadat.

Work section

A. Study the newspaper front page opposite, then answer these questions:
1. Explain the meaning of 'Sadat accepts Israel as a nation' (line 1).
2. In what way was this a major change in Middle Eastern affairs?
3. Judging by what you have read so far, what remained unchanged?
4. Suggest why Sadat thought his trip to Israel involved 'great risk' (last line).

B. Using the same headings as those in exercise A on page 23, show in two columns the similarities and differences between the 1956, 1967 and 1973 Arab–Israeli wars.

13

WAR IN LEBANON

Beirut 1976: a Muslim woman pleads with a Christian militiaman to spare her family's lives

Israel and Egypt made peace in 1979, but Israel's conflict with the other Arab states went on. The scene of the conflict in the early 1980s was Lebanon, the smallest of the Arab states around Israel.

Lebanon

Although small, Lebanon contains many ethnic and religious groups. The majority of Lebanese are Muslims, divided into three sects – Sunnis, Shi'ites and Druzes. Most of the others are Christians, divided into Maronites, Greek Orthodox and Greek Catholics. Throughout the twentieth century there has been conflict amongst these groups, especially between Maronite Christians and Sunni Muslims.

When Lebanon became independent in 1945 power was shared between these groups. The President was a Maronite, the Prime Minister a Sunni, and the Speaker of Parliament a Shi'ite. This arrangement worked well for several years, with each group trying to co-operate with the others. After 1948, however, the Arab–Israeli conflict made it difficult for them to work together. As you have read, in 1949 Lebanon had to make room for 100,000 Palestinian refugees fleeing from Israel. This upset the delicate balance of Lebanon's population.

Each Arab–Israeli war brought new problems to Lebanon. The Arab defeat in 1956 created unrest in many Arab countries, and in Lebanon this led to a civil war between Sunnis and Maronites. The Six Day War of 1967 increased the number of Palestinian refugees to 300,000 – a tenth of Lebanon's population – by 1970.

The PLO in Lebanon

It was not only the refugees who created problems. More important was the fact that the PLO came with them and set up bases in their camps. In south-east Lebanon the PLO had so many bases that the area was known as 'Fatahland'. In Beirut, where the PLO set up headquarters, five refugee camps provided bases for military training, recruiting and propaganda.

From 1968 onwards, PLO guerillas in Lebanon made daily attacks on Israel. The Israelis hit back with reprisal raids, the most spectacular being in 1968 when Israeli troops landed by helicopter at Beirut airport and blew up thirteen Lebanese airliners.

The Lebanese government could do nothing to stop the PLO from attacking Israel, for the Muslims in the government supported the PLO while the Maronites condemned them. Anyway, the Lebanese army was too small to take action against the PLO. So, from 1970 onwards, it allowed the PLO complete control of the refugee camps as well as the right to take part in 'armed struggle' against Israel.

As a result, the PLO continued to attack Israel throughout the 1970s. And for every PLO attack came an Israeli reprisal. After the deaths of the Israeli athletes at the Munich Olympics, for example, Israeli forces killed 118 people and dynamited 150 houses belonging to suspected PLO guerillas.

The Maronites refused to accept the power of the PLO in Lebanon and formed military groups such as the Phalangist Militia and Tiger Militia to oppose them. In reply, Shi'ite and Druze Muslims joined forces with the PLO. By 1975 the rival groups were fighting a full-scale civil war, with 40,000 people killed. Large areas of Beirut were destroyed. Hundreds of thousands of people lost their homes. The civil war came to a bloody end when the Syrian army invaded Lebanon and joined forces with the Christians. After defeating the PLO, the Syrians then turned on the Christians as well, killing thousands.

Israel and Lebanon

In March 1978, 26,000 Israeli troops invaded Lebanon after PLO guerillas killed Israeli civilians in a bus hijack. Their aim was to take control of southern Lebanon up to the Litani river in order to make it a 'buffer zone' protecting northern Israel.

In an attempt to restore peace, the United Nations sent a peace-keeping force to the area. The Israelis, however, did not trust the ability of the UN forces to protect their northern border. Instead, they allowed a Christian militia leader, Major Haddad, to control the border zone.

Neither the UN forces nor Major Haddad could stop the PLO from continuing their attacks. Israel responded in 1980–81 with heavy attacks on Lebanon until the UN organised a ceasefire in July 1981.

For nearly a year there was calm on the Israel–Lebanon border. But during that year the Israeli government made plans for a full-scale invasion of Lebanon. Their aim was to clear Lebanon of both PLO and Syrian forces, to destroy the PLO, to re-establish Christian rule throughout the country, and thus gain a more friendly neighbour.

In June 1982, 172,000 Israeli soldiers invaded Lebanon, bringing with them 3500 tanks and 600 fighter aircraft. The UN force patrolling the border did not have enough men or weapons to halt this invasion, and let the Israelis pass.

In order to keep their casualties to a minimum, the Israelis bombed towns on their route before entering them. The civilian casualties were therefore very high: 12,000 Lebanese were killed, 40,000 were wounded and 300,000 made homeless.

The killing went on after the Israelis reached Beirut, trapping the PLO there. The PLO, armed with anti-aircraft missiles and tanks, occupied residential areas of Beirut and fired on the Israelis from there. In reply, the Israeli air force bombed these areas, destroying apartment blocks, offices and even hospitals. Hundreds of civilians died in each raid.

Eventually the Israelis forced the PLO out of Beirut. Supervised by American troops, 13,000 armed PLO fighters left Beirut by ship for dispersal among Arab countries as far apart as Iraq and Algeria.

The defeat of Israel

Now that they had achieved their aim of driving the PLO out of Lebanon, things began to go wrong for the Israelis. In September 1982 the pro-Israeli, Maronite President Gemayel of Lebanon was killed in a massive bomb explosion in West Beirut. Israel's aim of gaining a friendly government was shattered.

Claiming that law and order had collapsed in West Beirut, Israel occupied the area and surrounded the Sabra-Chatila refugee camps where they claimed PLO guerillas were hiding. After sealing off the camps, the Israelis allowed gunmen from the Christian militias to search the camps for guerillas. The result was a massacre in which they killed some 2000 people, often after torturing and mutilating them.

The Sabra-Chatila massacre had the effect of turning many Israelis against the war in Lebanon. Some 400,000 joined an anti-war demonstration in Tel Aviv. Defence Minister Ariel Sharon resigned. Public opinion all over the world condemned Israel.

Israel began to withdraw its forces in 1983. American, French and Italian troops arrived to take their place in Beirut. In other areas that the Israelis left, Syrian troops occupied the land, along with the Shi'ite and Druze forces which they now backed.

As they retreated, the Israelis often came under attack from fanatical Shi'ites armed with suicide bombs. Dozens of Israeli soldiers died as young Shi'ites drove into army bases or convoys with huge quantities of explosive in their cars, and blew themselves up.

The last Israelis left Lebanon in April 1985. Behind them, Israeli workers dug a five-metre-wide ditch along the Lebanese border in an attempt to stop the Shi'ites bringing a new guerilla war into Israel. The Israelis had thus suffered their first defeat in the long conflict with Arabs in the Middle East.

Work section

A. Check your understanding of the forces involved in the Lebanon war by explaining the meanings of these names and words: Sunni; Shi'ite; Druze; Maronite; militias.

B. Study the photograph opposite. What does it reveal about the nature of the civil war in Lebanon?

C. Using the same headings as those in exercise A on page 23, show the similarities and differences between Israel's war in Lebanon, 1982–85, and the three previous Arab–Israeli wars.

THE CONFLICT SINCE 1985

Palestinian youths, led by a woman holding the out lawed Palestinian flag, demonstrate against the Israelis in the occupied West Bank area on 15 January 1989

The PLO after Lebanon

After leaving Beirut in 1982 the PLO quickly re-established itself as a political and military force. By 1986 PLO guerillas were back in south Lebanon and were again making cross-border attacks on Israel. As always, the Israeli armed forces carried out reprisal raids by bombing Lebanese cities and refugee camps.

The PLO had always contained splinter groups, such as Fatah (which took control of the organisation in 1969) and the PFLP. After the PLO left Lebanon, more splinter groups came into being. Some opposed Yassir Arafat because they thought he was too willing to enter peace negotiations and they carried on their own campaign of terror in the Middle East. In 1985, for example, the Palestine Liberation Front hijacked a cruise ship, the *Achille Lauro*, and the Abu Nidal group hijacked an Egyptian airliner.

One effect of this terror campaign was to spread the Arab–Israeli conflict into countries beyond the Middle East. Shootings and bombings took place in countries such as France and Britain as terrorists took revenge on their enemies. When, in 1986, an American soldier was killed by a terrorist bomb in West Berlin, the United States Air Force bombed the Libyan cities of Tripoli and Benghazi in order to destroy the bases in which they believed the terrorists had been trained. 130 people were killed in the American attack.

The war of the terrorist groups reached its furthest extremes in Lebanon, where the civil war that had started in 1975 continued. Groups such as the Islamic Jihad (Holy War) Organisation, the Hezbollah (Party of God), the Arab Red Knights and the Black Brigades fought each other in a bloody war which continued to disfigure the shattered city of Beirut. An increasingly important weapon in this terrorist war was the taking of hostages, usually foreigners, in order to put pressure on foreign governments.

Israel after the Lebanon War

After Israeli forces withdrew from Lebanon in 1985 the Israeli government made attempts to improve its relations with the Arab states. Prime Minister Shimon Peres had talks in Morocco with King Hassan and in Egypt with President Mubarak in 1986. He also settled a long-standing dispute with Egypt over who owned Taba, a small area in Sinai, by agreeing to let an international court decide the issue.

The Israeli government, however, was not united in this approach to the Arabs. After stalemates in elections in 1984, Israel's main political parties had shared power in a '**government of national unity**'. In this government, Shimon Peres, the left-wing Labour leader, took a turn as Prime Minister before handing over the post to the right-wing leader, Yitzhak Shamir, in 1986. Shamir was under pressure from his supporters not to negotiate with the Arabs over the future of the West Bank. Jewish settlers continued to build new villages there, despite the agreement made at Camp David to allow the West Bank Palestinians some rights of self-government. These settlers warned that they would oppose any attempt to do so, using violence and civil disobedience if necessary.

The *intifada*

Faced with such harsh attitudes, the 'government of national unity' found it impossible to satisfy the demands of both Israeli settlers and Palestinian Arabs. As a result, tension rose in the West Bank and Gaza during 1987. Demonstrations and protests by Arabs became everyday events. On 9 December 1987 demonstrators in Gaza attacked an Israeli army patrol, which shot two of them dead. Talks between senior Army officers and local Arab leaders failed to stop the demonstrations, which quickly turned into an *intifada*, the Arabic word for uprising.

The *intifada* spread rapidly throughout Gaza. In the refugee camps there, gangs of young Palestinians set up barricades of tyres, stones and corrugated iron, and ran the streets behind the barricades as 'no-go areas' closed to the army. As the uprising spread to the West Bank, Palestinians also mounted a campaign of strikes and economic boycotts. They refused to work for Israeli employers. Shopkeepers put up their shutters. Workers went on strike.

Some of the emotions involved in the uprising can be glimpsed in a best-selling song recorded in 1988 by Riyad Awad, Palestine's most popular singer:

A.   *Intifada*
    With petrol bomb and stone
    I will build my state,
    I will bear my revolution.
    May my strength increase.
    My land, my people,
    Strike with the stone.
    Burn, burn the tyre,
    Put up barriers.
    Revolution, revolution, do not fade.

The 'iron fist' policy

The Israeli government responded to the *intifada* with what Prime Minister Shamir called an 'iron fist' policy. The army used live ammunition as well as riot-control equipment to put down demonstrations. Thousands of young Palestinians were arrested and detained. Many were severely beaten with rifle butts and batons. Towns which took part in the uprising were put under curfew and the homes of riot leaders were demolished. Large numbers of schools were closed down, with the government claiming that they had become training centres for rioting youths.

The 'iron fist' policy produced many casualties. By the middle of 1989, 510 Palestinians had been killed and many thousands detained. With well-documented stories of Israeli brutality appearing in the foreign press, Israel was internationally condemned for the 'iron fist' policy. The UN Security Council condemned the army for violating human rights, while foreign governments issued public criticisms.

The new face of the PLO

With world opinion turning against Israel, the PLO suddenly attracted new sympathy for its cause by changing its tactics. Yassir Arafat, leader of the PLO, announced in November 1988 that they would no longer use terrorism in pursuit of their aims.

At the same time, the Palestine National Council, the PLO's parliament, proclaimed the creation of the independent State of Palestine, later appointing Arafat as President. Although the new state was only symbolic, for it controlled no territory, ninety countries gave it their official recognition. Support for the new state grew in 1989 when Arafat continued to speak in moderate tones of negotiating a settlement with Israel. Even the USA, Israel's staunchest ally, took part in talks with representatives of the PLO.

Israel under pressure

Under attack from the international community as well as from the Palestinians, the Israeli government tried to win back support by putting forward a peace plan in 1989. Prime Minister Shamir proposed to hold elections in the occupied territories to choose Palestinian 'go-betweens' who would negotiate with Israel some form of self-government for their people. However, right-wing members of Shamir's Likud party were appalled by his willingness to negotiate with the PLO. They forced him to add such strict conditions to the plan that the PLO rejected it.

In the Likud and other right-wing parties, some Israelis now talked of extreme solutions such as annexing the occupied territories to make them fully part of Israel. Jewish settlers in the occupied territories formed vigilante groups to attack Palestinian rebels. Clashes between Jews and Arabs increased in number and severity. All the while, the continuing *intifada* kept Israel in a state of permanent crisis.

As the 1980s drew to a close, therefore, the long-running conflict in Palestine seemed as far from a just and lasting settlement as it had ever been.

Work section

A. Study the photograph opposite.
  1. Suggest why the Israelis used an 'iron fist' policy to deal with disturbances such as this.
  2. Using your imagination, suggest other ways of dealing with such disturbances.
  3. What would have been the advantages and disadvantages to the Israeli government of using the methods you have suggested?

B. Look back to Chapter 4 on pages 8 to 9.
  1. What similarities are there between events in Palestine in 1937–39 and in Israel in 1987–89?
  2. How do the two sets of events differ?

C. Study the song in source A above.
  1. In general, what uses can a historian make of popular songs?
  2. How might a historian in fifty years time use source A in a study of the *intifada*?
  3. What would be the limitations of using source A in the ways you have suggested?

Revision guide

You may find it helpful to make notes on what you have read in Part Two of this book. If you are unsure how to organise them, this list of headings shows the main points to note. They follow on from those on page 14.

G. The uneasy peace, 1949–55
1. The armistice agreements of 1949
2. The growth of the new state of Israel
3. Changes in the Arab world
4. The Fedayeen
5. Economic warfare against Israel

H. The Suez–Sinai War of 1956
1. Causes of the war
2. Events of the war
3. Results of the war.

I. The reshaping of the Middle East, 1956–67
1. Changes in the Arab states
2. The United Arab Republic
3. Creation of the PLO
4. Fatah
5. Changes in Israel

J. The Six Day War of 1967
1. Causes of the war
2. Events of the war
3. Results of the war

K. War by other means, 1967–73
1. Resolution 242
2. The war of attrition, 1969–70
3. The PLO and the guerilla war

L. The Yom Kippur War of 1973
1. Causes of the war
2. Events of the war
3. Results of the war

M. Moves towards peace, 1973–79
1. The disengagement of forces, 1974
2. Sadat's peace initiative, 1977
3. The Camp David peace talks, 1978
4. The Washington Treaty, 1979

N. War in Lebanon
1. Lebanon's ethnic and religious groups
2. The refugee problem in Lebanon
3. The PLO in Lebanon
4. The civil war in Lebanon, 1975–76
5. Israeli attacks on Lebanon, 1978–81
6. Israel's war in Lebanon, 1982–85
   - The invasion
   - The attack on Beirut
   - The PLO leaves Beirut
   - The Sabra-Chatila massacre
   - The Israeli withdrawal from Lebanon

O. The conflict since 1985
1. The PLO after Lebanon
2. Israel since 1985
3. The intifada
4. The 'iron fist' Policy.

Revision exercise

Some aspects of the Arab–Israeli conflict have changed since 1948. Other aspects have changed very little. Using the following titles, show in two columns headed *Continuity* and *Change* which aspects of the conflict have changed and which have not.
- Involvement of the superpowers (USA and USSR)
- Arab governments' attitudes to Israel
- Guerilla warfare against Israel
- Conditions of the Palestinian refugees (for example living conditions, political rights)
- Conditions of Israelis
- Leadership of the Arab world
- Involvement of the United Nations
- Methods of war

Example:	*Continuity*	*Change*
Arab governments' attitudes to Israel	Hostile. Continuing refusal to recognise the existence of Israel	Egypt recognised Israel after the Camp David Agreement in 1978